LOVE'S CONTAGION

WHO DO YOU REALLY BELIEVE IN?

ROGER GRAINGER

Order this book online at www.trafford.com
or email orders@trafford.com

Most Trafford titles are also available at major online book retailers.

The Scripture quotations used herein are from the *New Revised Standard
Version of the Bible*, Copyright © 1989, by the Division of Christian
Education of the National Council of the Churches of Christ in the
United States of America. Used by permission. All rights reserved.

Printed in the United States of America.

ISBN: 978-1-4907-3464-4 (sc)
ISBN: 978-1-4907-3465-1 (e)

Trafford rev. 04/30/2014

www.trafford.com
North America & international
toll-free: 1 888 232 4444 (USA & Canada)
fax: 812 355 4082

CONTENTS

Our vision of the truth has to be big enough to include other people's truth as well as our own. Let us continue to hold together at our deepest level. We are a forgiven community.
Beth Allen, 1984
(Religious Society of Friends (Quakers) in Britain, 2013, 10.28)

CHAPTER 1

'My mother was always very religious.'

Some people think of religion as an obsession, an idea which a person cannot get rid of. Other see it as a neurosis, a useful way of shielding the self against adversity by learning to interpret it in a way which deflects it or, at least, is capable of lessening the impact it has upon us. Alternatively, it can be seen as an effective way of dealing with feelings of guilt, either rational or otherwise; accepting religious feelings as justified relieves this kind of psychological pressure. This is a very short list of the things which religion is able to do for, or with, us—limiting itself to those which function at an unconscious or semi-automatic level. They are some of the ways in which religious people tend to be understood by their fellow human beings and deserve to be taken into consideration by those at whom they are aimed; even though they are felt to miss the mark, they are recognised as valuable *because* they do this.

Certainly religion has other more public functions. For instance, those 'unofficial,' or unacknowledged, characteristics may be consciously manipulated by others for purposes of direction and control. This is a fact about religion which its critics find extremely useful—and who can blame them? Sometimes the result has been, and continues to be, politically disastrous and, even when this is not the case, the means employed for peace-keeping involve a good deal of stress on the need for obedience to authority and the strict use of religious sanctions of various kinds. At a less dramatic level, fear of punishment, sometimes human but more frequently divine, plays a notable part in the religious awareness of many who have been brought up to fear the spiritual authority of the priesthood. In the words of the young James Joyce's spiritual directors,

> No king or emperor of the earth has the power of
> the priest of God (Joyce, 1960, 158).

All the same this is not a book about the misuse of authority. Nor is it about neurosis. Its concern is with whatever it may be that we consider important enough to afford the highest place in our lives, elevating it far about everything else. These are the things we hold as our personal, final truth about life. The need to find expressive words remains the same, although the story told may be very different. A contemporary writer describes two contrasting 'explanations of ultimacy':

> One person looks around and sees a universe created by a god who watches over its long unfurling, marking the fall of sparrows and listening to the prayers of his finest creation. Another person believes that life in all its baroque complexity is a chemical aberration that will briefly decorate the surface of a ball of rock spinning somewhere among a billion galaxies (Haddon, 2013, 199).

The second of these two accounts scarcely qualifies as religious and actually goes out of its way in order not to do so; yet the enthusiasm with which it is presented and the conviction to which it bears witness give it an almost credal significance, according it the dignity which attaches to scientific pronouncements of all kinds. Certainly the second version creates a sense of wonder which the first may seem to have forfeited by relying on metaphor to capture something that otherwise would remain inexpressible, a way of avoiding our duty to subject anything to its lowest common denominator. Metaphors can never be measured but the origin of the universe, well, who knows? To call a scientific theory a creed is definitely figurative. On the other hand, this is a kind of metaphor which scientists themselves frequently use when the reality which they are describing lies beyond the reach of the kind of language they are dedicated to using. In large areas of the world, the non-literal sense of the word 'God' is part of people's ordinary vocabulary as they express themselves on matters about which they feel strongly or seek to describe an experience which they regard as extraordinary, particularly one which they were unprepared for and which took them by surprise. 'God' is frequently invoked in this way by believers and non-believers alike, not as someone with whom we have a personal relationship but as an exalted official, or Higher Civil Servant, responsible for ensuring that things turn out the way we expect and that no-one 'upsets the apple cart.'

This kind of behaviour is common among human beings who, whether or not they actually believe in God, still find it convenient, when the occasion arises, to treat him in such a way. We know from what Jesus tells us that familiarity with him is to be encouraged, this being precisely what he wants; but we should take more care not to allow it to degenerate into the disdain we sometimes feel for those who wound our own self-esteem. If we believe that God is love, and have personally experienced him to be such, we should make more effort to treat him as our lover and not simply as 'the one in charge.' For us, as human beings, 'all-loving' is more important than 'all-powerful.' Far more important . . .

The important thing, then, is love: love as the gift which God gives so that we can give it back, both to one another and to him—particularly to him for he is the source of the love we live by sharing. This is the responsive love in which we turn to whomever or whatever is not ourself in order to share his gift with them—the gift which he continues to bestow because it is who he *is*. It is hard to find words for this because the experience is not one to be caught and held, although the doctrinal statements have the power to keep on reminding us of it, of the experience of losing and finding the God whom our hearts love, he who summons us away from ourselves to find him where we had not expected.

This, then, is the underlying theme of this book: God's intention for his creation, lived out in time and eternity, is to be himself for us. This means enabling us to allow ourselves to be loved. 'Love your neighbour as yourself,' Jesus says; love is not to be hoarded. Indeed, it cannot be as it lives in exchange—or more precisely in *interchange*. It comes home to us in being given away by us, so that it is always among us as evidence of its origin. We may tell ourselves that God's love is different from ours but this is because of our tendency to see love itself as something that belongs to us, which we can use as we see fit, apportioning it according to other people's merit or, worse, trying to use it as a way of earning the love which they themselves would otherwise withhold from us. We treat loving as a kind of commercial activity, something to be bought and sold. Perhaps we may try to reassure ourselves with the thought that, after all, such an attitude is entirely suitable for life in the world in which we live which depends so much on principles of 'give and take.'

God's love, on the other hand, is ideal rather than practical, although we are reasonably certain that it functions on much the same lines. Certainly we are able to conceive of his being more forgiving than we usually are and that, when he does punish, it really is for our own good and should not be confused with a human desire for vengeance. Because we are human it is perfectly understandable that we should feel the need to create a god in our own image and that this is the god we should worship; what is certainly true, however, is that this god is not he who is revealed to us—and who continues to show his true self at work in his world. It is not that God's love is different but that love itself is other than we have sometimes supposed it to be.

Julius of Norwich has this to say on the subject of punishment: 'God regards sin as sorrow and pain for his lovers to whom, for love, he assigns no blame.' No blame but only love. Ian Suttie, the celebrated Scottish psychiatrist, saw hate and the human desire to inflict punishment as the frustrated aspect of love, as 'tails' is the obverse of 'heads' in the same penny. Suttie goes on to say that, in his view, 'the whole story of the crucifixion illustrates free forgiving, on the understanding that hate and evil *have no independent existence*, but are merely the frustration-forms of love itself, distorted as protest, reproach and that kind of aggression which is originally intended to compel attention' (1988, 142). Hate then comes from an intense desire to be loved.

But this is not the way in which God loves us. It is easy enough to spoil love by not allowing it to carry out its task which is to grow. Love needs room for spreading, for reaching out and touching others, thus infecting them with itself. Love brings

5

together; to make it exclusive is to get in its way. This is what happens when we use the impulse to love in order to divide, contrast, discriminate which, as human beings, is our preferred way of making sense of life. It is the way we naturally think and talk, in stories to one another and to ourselves, and as we tell them we move back into them and take up residence, collating them with the stories others tell us about themselves. This is not so when we manage to think of god, consciously giving him permission to come into our minds. Our participation in his glory is not in judging and comparing, in struggling to work things out for ourselves, but simply in replying to his address, allowing his Being to touch our own.

It is then, as Jesus says, that we discover yet again our own preciousness to God, when we loose ourselves from our anxieties and preoccupations and lose ourselves in Being:

> Look at the birds of the air; they neither sow nor
> reap nor gather into barns, and yet your heavenly
> Father feels them (Mt 6.26).

Even now, when psychologists have devised effective ways of increasing the mind's ability to deal with the anxieties of being human, this is by no means an easy thing to do. Even if we learn techniques for clearing our minds from the pressure of surface anxieties, there are things which lie deeper than this, burdens of which we are not fully aware, although we are certainly conscious of their effects on our lives. This is why Jesus speaks of faith— faith as the ability to be ourselves in the way our Father in heaven would have us be.

Faith is nothing less than loving and allowing ourselves to be loved, the two aspects of the Love which created us and holds us in being. Our human problem lies in not knowing what to do with the love which we both have and are, particularly if we allow other things—fear, for example, and shame, a sense of weakness and vulnerability—to get in the way. With God there is only love. With us it is different. Our loving is two faced: those who love intensely will hate in the same measure if their love is blocked. This is the case whether they turn their rage and frustration against a person or a thing or reserve it for themselves. They may in fact project it onto god because, after all, he it is who first gave them the power to love and now it must surely be he who is frustrating it. As Congreve puts it, 'Heaven has no rage like love to hatred turned' (1697, Act III, Scene VIII). For us, love can be dangerous. It is easy for it to show its other face.

Projecting on god like this turns him into a sadistic tyrant who does not care for his people and turns away from those who cry out to him for help. We are told that we should bring our lives into his presence and are met with pain and disappointment when we do this. Informed about the value of suffering, we remain unconvinced. Looking for someone to return our love, all we can find is ourselves. We tell ourselves this is enough—after all, it is the only person we are willing to let ourselves recognise—but we remain unconvinced. How can we be if we are determined not to see God as he is, as he is for us—not in our thinking *about* him but in our experience *of* him. As the prayer says, 'our hearts are restless till they find their rest in thee,' words which have been borrowed from St Augustine's *Confessions* (Church of England. Liturgical Commission, 1999, Collect for 17th Sunday after Trinity).

Regarding God as over against us rather than alive among us allows us easily to react towards him as cruel parent rather than loving Father. Both in a religious and a human sense, closeness to the person who nurtures and protects us is vital. From the very beginning of our life, Bowlby says,

> No form of behaviour is accompanied by stronger
> feeling than is attachment behaviour. The figures
> to whom it is directed are loved and their advent
> is greeted with joy. So long as a child is in the
> unchallenged presence of a principle attachment figure,
> or within easy reach, he feels secure (1971, 257).

The unchallenged presence: in a sense, this can only mean God. For human beings, loving and the security which it brings never goes unthreatened. Another analyst, Ian Suttie (1988), writes about the fear of loving, of willingly giving oneself to someone else, because of the surrender it is perceived as entailing. The unassailed human soul fears the price it would have to pay if love were to be rejected or abused. The two things go together, as it is the need for security which both drives us forward and holds us back. God, for those who believe in him, overcomes this by loving us in a way which gives us the courage to respond without fear. Without help the soul finds the task of being its own divinity beyond its powers and seeks a way out by settling for a less demanding kind of involvement.

Responsiveness, however, is the gift of God who empowers us if we are willing to allow him. It is the total, unchallenged nature of his giving that is able to answer our fearfulness. Religious people give it theological names—such as Holy Spirit—which by their association with real personal experience of relationship to Otherness take on a particular resonance as evidence of reaching out and being found, or at least rediscovered. This responsiveness is both gift and possession. We recognise ourselves as those able to reciprocate a concern which is our fulfilment, a loving which is always and essentially a *sharing*. All this happens when we are able to restrain ourselves from taking charge, or trying to do so, in order to angle the exchange exclusively in a direction chosen by ourselves which may very well not be the most loving one. Here, the advice offered by Teilhard de Chardin holds good with regard to the leading of Holy Spirit.

> Only God could say what this new spirit gradually forming within you will be. Give Our Lord the benefit of believing that his hand is leading you, and accept the anxiety of feeling yourself in suspense and incomplete (Teilhard de Chardin in Harter, 2005).

The sense of being led by a spirit which is both personal and transcendental, which is present to us and at the same time inescapably beyond us, is characteristic of many religions, perhaps even of religion itself. Analytical psychology speaks of the soul as 'an energetic emergent entity' (Bishop, 2013, 23) and Christian theology relates it to the Image of God which lives on in his human creation, working ceaselessly to transform human life in the world—not only souls but bodies as well.

The Image of God, then, is not simply an idea or a pious aspiration. It is a human fact of life—ourselves body and soul expressing God's intention for us to live in communion with him and one another, to be like him in human mode.

> St Bernard says that, whereas the soul of man was made in the Image of God, his body was fashioned in the image of his soul, and that is why we stand erect. The soul's erectness, however, has been lost

9

> by sin; man is now *curvus*, bent in respect of his
> spirit, for the Image of God in which it was made is
> defaced. Of that fact, his still upright body reminds
> him ceaselessly (Sister Penelope, 1974, 5).

For Christians, human beings are always 'body and soul,' the former a continuing reminder of the latter, there to turn our attention to its shortcomings apart from Christ Jesus, our embodied Lord. Just as our bodies long for a state of complete physical composure, a condition of organic balance and freedom from pain, so our souls yearn for God.

This is the kind of soul and body holism which Jung identified as the essential characteristic of all human beings. For the great Austrian analyst, the soul was the body's hallmark, its mean of authentification, just as our physical presence stands as guarantee of our essential spirituality which we share with the entire human race.

> It is, to my mind, a fatal mistake to consider the
> human psyche as a merely personal affair, and to
> explain it exclusively from a person point of view
> (Jung, 1938, 16).

Jung declares quite straightforwardly that the capacity for religious belief is 'an illimitable and undefinable addition to every personality' (1938, 47). This, he says, is something which resists attempts at explanation in scientific or rationalistic terms, claiming that 'dogma expresses an irrational entity through the image' (1938, 56).

It is because these things are, to the scientific mind, 'irrational' that they are so important. Jung's painstaking investigation of the quality of human experience convinces him of the limitations of scientific approaches to understanding people. Although he himself did not subscribe to any actual religion, he values religion higher than any attitude of mind which denies the significance to the reality to which it points and claims it as an illusion. For Jung religion is the cure of neurosis rather than—as has sometimes been claimed—simply a form of it.

> And if such experience helps to make your life healthier, more beautiful, more complete and more satisfactory to yourself and to those whom you love, you may safely say "This was the grace of God" (1938, 114).

From this point of view, then, religious awareness is mediated to each individual by our unconscious psychic co-inheritance which is the source of the images of God we call upon. The bible uses language of a different kind, taken from a precise account of a race of men and women whom God has created in order to be members of his own personal family. Certainly for 'people of the book' the idea of basing knowledge of God on the collective unconscious, even when this is explained as the origin of every kind of human understanding, 'whether of heaven or earth,' lacks the spiritual impact of the Genesis story but, as Jung himself is eager to stress, his formulation tries hard to look at religion from the standpoint of 'psychological science'—something which religion itself never does, which is precisely the point he is making. Of all ways of expressing the dynamic nature of our unconscious life religious symbolism is the most psychologically accurate for, 'The dogma represents the soul more completely than a scientific theory' (Jung, 1938, 57).

It is in this inner sense of God's presence as ungraspable, dynamic, life-creating that the Image of God subsists. There is nothing vague or elusive about it. It speaks, acts, thinks and moves using space and time to do so. With regard to human awareness it is at work in the space between thought and thought, intuitively, as faith—the knowledge which precedes argument. It is God's image and, as such, it cannot be done away with. In the words of a contemporary American theologian, 'The act of being human is unrelentingly in relationship with God.' He goes on to say that, although human sin perverts the relationship, it has never managed to destroy it; how could it do so if God has created us for—and within—it? 'As a creation or gift from God, humanness cannot be annulled or rescinded except if God were to do it' (Woolridge, 2013, 35). Christ's incarnation shows God's purpose to be strikingly different; in Jesus we can recognise our true identity in spite of the self-centred arrogance which obscures it. In Christ the Divine Image shines and clearly draws us to rediscover the love with which God the Father binds us to himself. The Anglican Collect for the First Sunday of Christmas expresses this clearly for us

> Almighty God, who wonderfully created us in your own image and yet more wonderfully restored us through your Son Jesus Christ: grant that, as he came to share in our humanity, so we may share the life of his divinity; (Church of England. Liturgical Commission, 1999, 381)

As Jesus says to his disciples, 'Whoever sees me sees him who sent me' (Jn 12:44). In Christ the Image of God is restored as a restorer renews a painting: the work exists, it has not been destroyed. In the same way, our ability to 'see' spiritually is occluded by sin but never completely taken away. If it were, how could we ever see? How could we ever be brought to see clearly again?

The above is written from a specific point of view and represents my own personal frame of mind as a Christian. My opinion on the matter of how human beings stand with God obviously differs from someone whose conclusions are based solely on empirical, scientifically testable evidence, so that he or she has learned to dismiss data of other kinds, particularly information which claims to proceed from a dimension that is specifically defined as 'beyond all measure.' All the same, it seems likely that those who believe in God, whatever their religion may officially be, are aware of an important connection between his Being and their own existence. This may be expressed in dogmatic form, but the connection is not actually theoretical. In other words, the life of the relationships is not formal but personal and what we have learned about its nature stays with us only to the extent that it chimes with a presence of which we are continually aware. Doctrines about God—about what he is to *us*—serve as *aides-memoires*, reminders of a fact about ourselves with which we are over-familiar, the reality of a God whom we know, yet take for granted. In this sense, we recognise God's presence within a written text of a familiar ritual, not because he has taken up residence there but because this is the place where he has arranged to meet us. We have treasured personal experience of such encounters and we long to repeat them.

CHAPTER 2

'Our hearts are restless . . .' Up to now we have been talking mainly about people who own up to being religious in the sense of actually believing in God. The main argument of this book is that many consciously yearn for spiritual fulfilment who would certainly disavow any attachment to religious belief. For them, those who believe in God do so because they have a particular type of mind which makes them a special kind of person. Perhaps they have been indoctrinated during their formative years; possibly they are actually born in this way, having inherited it from their parents. One thing is reasonably certain and that is that they cannot be very intelligent or they would realise how stupid it is to believe in something for which there is so very little real evidence—unless, of course, like James Joyce's clergy, they happen to have an ulterior motive.

But is believing in God so ridiculous? Philosophers have argued that it is a natural thing for us to do. They have said that it is something which belongs to the nature and identity of men and women, so that the task of philosophy is to demonstrate human freedom by arguing *against* it. The truth is, they say, that believing in God is a characteristic of being human and needs no defence. Carry on arguing, they say, because that is human too . . . John Calvin was so certain of the naturalness of our awareness of God that he wrote about the *semen religionis*: 'God has sown a seed of religion in all men' (McNeill, 2011, I, III, 1). This is a Christian version of a creation story belonging to all three 'religions of the book,' to Judaism and Islam as well as Christianity. Indeed, the belief that human beings are descended from god-figures is common to many religions throughout the world where the creators of the universe also function as 'fecundators' (Jn 14:7-11; Col 1:15-20; 1 Jn 3:2; Eliade, 1958).

It is not surprising, then, if at some level of awareness there is a feeling of kinship, as if we are made in such a way that we can somehow sense God's presence without consciously acknowledging that this is what is happening to us (Plantigna, 1981, 46). Thus, as Jung says, symbols of divinity are made real for us at an unconscious level. If we love the natural world, we are used to places and times which move us in ways it is difficult to describe. We talk about being 'uplifted' and describe being overcome with feelings of awe; yet it is not what we see that amazes us but our own unexpected reaction to it.

> I'm not a religious man by any means but there have been occasions while climbing in some of the mountainous parts of the world when I have surprised myself by suddenly feeling a sense of awe and mystery, of being in the presence of something beyond my grasp. I have only felt this rarely and only in the mountains (Anon: Personal communication).

The man who wrote this is an experienced mountaineer but he is describing a sensation with which many are familiar, although it tends to be one which only nature poets like Wordsworth and his fellow Romantics appear to take very seriously, perhaps because common sense assures the rest of us that the scenery, which we find so moving and inspiring, is not actually responsible for the effect it has upon us. It is 'we ourselves' who feel these things, not the breathtaking panorama into which we have stumbled. Psychologists of human perception assure us that we create our own landscapes out of the materials which are available to us.

Nevertheless, those who have experienced these things themselves tend to be unwilling to dismiss them out of hand. Somehow they leave their mark on us. Christians would argue that it is not unreasonable to expect that the divinity we are called to recognise in one another should somehow leave its mark on other things as well; more to the point, if we are inherently capable of sensing God's activity in the things which go on happening to us, then we should not be surprised to find evidence of him in the material world in which we all think, feel and behave to one another. This is the world of human perception in which God has chosen to take up residence with us. This is not an insight which is confined to Christianity, despite the fact that among Christians other forms of religious belief which draw on our perception of the natural world are customarily dismissed as 'nature-worship.' 'People of the Book,' whether Jewish, Christian or Muslim, share a horror of anything which seems to savour of idolatry, despite the story of Yahweh's addressing Moses from the heart of the burning bush (Ex 3). Certainly it was not the bush itself that Moses worshipped, any more than the traveller considers the actual mountain to be in any way divine or supernatural.

Here, of course, the power of imagination plays a crucial role in widening the scope of perception. In imagination subject and object come together, the first allowing itself to trust the unreality which lies before it, the second arranging for that same unreality to assume an emotional resonance which atones for its fictional identity. Pythagoras' Theorem and *The Tempest* are both true but with different kinds of truth, one cognitive, the other emotional. The cognitive truth of story depends on its function of presenting an account of events which corresponds to the way in which human beings organise their thoughts in order to make sense of whatever is happening, an operation which involves taking a sample of thoughts, feelings and events which can be made to take on the consistency of an articulated happening, something which possesses a beginning, a middle and an end, the shape of the conclusions we draw about things. The emotional truth depends on the congruence between story and cognitive process, which makes the people and events portrayed seem real enough to be taken seriously and allows us to exercise the feelings which events and people bring to life in the world outside the story. Because we know it is a story we are able to go along with the process of becoming psychologically involved, identifying our own experience of life with that of the characters in the story.

Our commitment to religion has a great deal to do with our tendency to immerse ourselves in story. This is because, as a medium, a way of communicating ideas and feelings, story is unsurpassed. In itself it is a symbol of recognisable and therefore *shareable* experience. However diffuse or even long-winded it may appear, it possesses the shape of conviction. 'What I tell you three times is true,' says Lewis Carroll's Bellman (Carroll, 1876). Each movement, beginning, middle and end, is an inseparable part of the whole, being essential for its meaning and yet the whole stands as a completed action, a statement which carries conviction signified by its threefold nature—three being, as Euclid says, 'the sign of perfection.'

It is the mark of intention, of something definitely stated. That does not mean it is always true, however. Far from it. Story establishes a position, opening it up for either confirmation or contradiction, engagement or rebuttal. We are invited to regard it as a message, on the understanding that whether we accept or reject it is to be left completely up to ourselves. To us it may strike home as true or false, something to be accepted or rejected, loved or simply ignored. As I have said elsewhere, this is true of all stories, not only ones with an obvious meaning and whose message is explicit, like the Good Samaritan or the Prodigal Son. All stories are not intended as parables, conveying a serious truth about life and death, but they each communicate a message, however trivial the subject may be, which has been encapsulated in story form to signify that it is complete enough to stand by itself.

The importance of story for a message which is not simply taught but embedded in a birth, life and death stands out exceptionally clearly. Religious people are 'converts to a story,' one which tells of encountering God and being part of the narrative he is creating, one which gives life and meaning. In some cases, it is a story specifically about himself, which is the most powerful of all ways in which he grasps our imagination, because we find ourselves already taking part in what he is revealing to us, already characters in his drama. Our knowledge of God is the circumstance which renders story-telling itself precious as our own experience of him reaches for the clarity which only stories have at their disposal. This is something we shall return to later.

We should be careful then, when we dismisses something as 'only a story,' particularly as the phrase is so often taken to mean something specially invented for the occasion but which has no permanent truthfulness, being simply 'made up.' This is not necessarily the case with personal testimony, of course, but generally speaking in many areas of life stories are considered to be a second rate kind of truth. With stories about the underlying meaning and purpose of life, however, the juxtaposition of truth and fiction turns out to be irrelevant as actual events, occurring within measurable time, are infused with a timelessness perceived as being 'outside' time altogether. All the same, they continue to exist as real happenings, things 'true' to nature because that is where they took place. Profound spiritual truths authenticate time-bound existence by revealing its true identity as belonging to a wider truthfulness, an ultimate story-telling.

Story makes use of our human ability to imagine completeness. As such it is the basis of both art and science, although scientists prefer to talk about theories, preferably ones which can be tested. Artists, too, have ways of deciding what constitutes authenticity, although these are qualitative, not quantitative; even so they possess the shape of some kind of realised statement, as something detached from everything else in order to stand by itself, signalling, 'I am here! What am I? How do you take me?'—using the same threefold configuration as a scientific proposition, in this case a movement from an idea to a statistically tested conclusion via an intervening theoretical hypothesis.

The urge to understand the world we live in, to weigh our conclusions about it, and the part which story plays in this, are characteristic functions of humanness. They are part of the language which we use to explore the terms of our existence as individuals and groups of people. Because they govern the way in which we think and feel and provide us with the means for managing our relationship with everything which affects our lives, it is not surprising that they should provide the means whereby we express our sense of things which lie outside the range of ordinary sense perception. Because we exchange stories about ourselves, we are not confused by God's revealing himself to us in the same way. Although this may sound vaguely blasphemous to some people, it should be pointed out that both Immanuel Kant and St Thomas Aquinas shared similar views, St Thomas maintaining that God's human image was to be found in the faculty of rational communication.

From this point of view, knowledge of God is equated with understanding his message, accepting its truth and acting in accordance with it. In other words, our way of understanding him corresponds to the knowledge of the way our minds work, a reasonable assumption seeing he himself designed them. A good many religious people seem convinced by the logic of this argument, claiming that, for human beings, God is the god of rationality, teaching us through his Spirit to understand how things fit together. We learn how things around us work because, like God, we are *makers*. The Image is that of the 'Divine Artificer' of eighteenth century theology. For others, however, such a way of understanding God is not only inadequate but misleading, the first because it engages with only one aspect of the way God is experienced in individual lives and the second because it encourages us to imagine that God could be reduced to a single one of his attributes—with the exception of love which defies reductionism of any kind and always will do!

God is actually experienced as a widening as opposed to any kind of narrowing, which is why he resists our attempts to tie him down by somehow managing to sum him up. How could it be otherwise? Renewed in Christ, we remain his creatures, formed by love in its own image, made by God in his likeness so that the love which lives in interchange could grow between ourselves and him—an answering love which shows its face in betweenness and the urge to share. If we have to locate God's image in ordinary human living, if we need to deify anything we perceive regarding ourselves, it should be the God-given ability to exchange love. Love creates space in our lives and the world in which we live. It is easy to let it be crowded out, registering its presence and then allowing ourselves to be distracted by the pressures of the world.

Perhaps there is a connection between the spiritual space which love creates and the sense of God's presence in deserted places such as wilderness landscapes and mountain peaks. 'The world is too much with us,' wrote William Wordsworth. 'Getting and spending we lay waste our powers' (1970, 117). Wordsworth is only one of many poets who have written about their experience of sensing God's presence in nature, outstanding among them Gerard Manley Hopkins and R. S. Thomas. Hopkins is perhaps the most explicit of them:

> The world is charged with the grandeur of God.
> It will flame out like shook foil (Hopkins, 1996, 14).

Wordsworth's specific message, however, concerns the way in which this brightness is occluded by things we allow to get in the way, notably our compulsion to see satisfaction in possessions as a way of bolstering our human vulnerability by 'giving ourselves away' in exchange for something more solid. Wordsworth describes this as a 'sordid boon,' sordid because it is in fact no more than a confidence trick. The implication here is that we would do better to bestow ourselves elsewhere, as our fulfilment lies in another direction than the market place.

For many people, then, religion is to be regarded as in more than one sense 'natural' to human beings. It is one of the characteristics of existence which has personal significant in terms of either acceptance or rejection, or both, for the experience of being undecided in the matter is actually as common as any kind of commitment, either for or against. I use the word 'commitment' rather than 'belief' or even 'opinion.' To be religious or not is more than simply making some kind of judgement regarding religion. Indeed, the testimony of those involved in teaching theology is that being interested in religious thinking, feeling and behaving on the part of others need not necessarily be evidence of awareness of being a religious person oneself. Religion always calls for a degree of personal commitment to its own world of thought and feeling in order to be identified as genuinely itself.

This does not mean, of course, that nothing *about* religion may be known by those who are not themselves religious but simply that religion itself is beyond their understanding. For one thing, like other human experiences it must be perceived as different from anything else in order to stand out and be identified as itself rather than a particular form of something else. For instance, it is common enough for religion to be explained as an unconscious control mechanism operating in order to inhibit the activities of the equally unconscious pleasure principle or, alternatively, as the product of intense social feeling. In other words, religion's purpose is either to disarm feeling (Freud) or to empower it (Durkheim). In either case, it is to be interpreted as something which is actually the epiphenomenon of something else, which explains how it comes to be used in ways which are diametrically opposed to each other!

Religion, the human perception of the reality which is God, is never anything other than itself. Certainly it may be encumbered in varying degrees of intensity or at various stages of its own readiness to receive it, but it is never an experience pointing away from itself, a conscious or unconscious reminder of something else. As we have seen, it uses story but is not in itself a story, even though stories may be the most effective, and the most truthful, ways of helping us to draw conclusions about the relationship between ourselves and God, which is something they try hard, and yet fail, to describe. If poets manage to do so, this is because they abandon the attempt at literal or scientific conformity with their subject, hoping, by creeping up at an angle, to take it, and us, by surprise:

> Tell all the truth but tell it slant,
> Success in circuit lies,
> Too bright for our infirm delight (Dickinson, 1970,
> 506).

It should be pointed out, however, that this is a way of registering religious experience, opening it out to others, not the way in which any of us actually feel it ourselves, which is personal and private, not to be known by anyone other than ourselves. 'That's between God and me,' we say. What we can do by our poetic attempts to capture this experience is simply nudge others in the direction of their own. As William James pointed out over a century ago, in its essential identity, religion is a private concern. Psychologically speaking, it corresponds to

> the feelings, acts and experiences of individual men
> in their solitude, so far as they apprehend themselves
> to stand in relation to the divine (1929, 31).

James goes on to say that the actual word 'religion' may be taken to mean more than this but whatever else it signifies may be traced back to the individual experience of men, women and children who may or may not make it explicit. When they do, they naturally join up with others to do the same and religion may be recognised as a social fact—but only when the individuals concerned have identified it as a private one. This is not to say, of course, that the presence of others willing to confess their religious feelings openly is not an important part in bringing them to conscious awareness within the individual, for religion is contagious at a human level, whether or not this fact is attributed to a divine cause.

This book follows James in concerning itself with the workings of religious states of mind rather than the specific teachings of particular groups of religious people on the subject of 'faith and practice' or the ways in which such groups are organised. We shall certainly be concerned here with religious behaviour but from the point of view of the human awareness which gives rise to it and sustains the forms it takes, all of which are aspects of the dramatic story in which truth is crystallised into words and images which speak the language of personal experience. As we saw earlier, the story is of crucial importance for our understanding. The story of our religion enshrines the image of our meeting with God himself; it is because of this that we find ourselves turning to it again and again in order to receive spiritual refreshment and guidance.

The story, in all its life-giving richness, is of crucial importance. In a sense, however, it remains secondary. Looking more closely at actual human experience we should perhaps be more honest about ourselves! Do we become religious through being convinced by a sacred text or an answered prayer, not having known any kind of religion before? Or does this life-changing event answer questions already deep within the soul, a searching not yet satisfied? Are we religious because we are moved or moved because we are religious?

The truth certainly appears to be that in fact both are the case, the first by virtue of our commitment to a story or abstraction, the second according to a powerful psychological predisposition which takes the form of a question to be asked, an emptiness to be filled. There is, however, no opposition in this for, as St Paul and William James agree, it is actually the story which answers the question.

CHAPTER 3

Up to now we have been assuming that religion itself originates in a spiritual longing expressed in a desire to worship God. This is not necessarily the same thing as belonging to an actual religion; indeed, some of those who are most conscious of its presence in themselves prefer not to mention it, choosing to distance themselves from those who do and talking of 'childish superstition' or even Obsessive Compulsive Disorder. Those who profess that they belong to a religious group attract scorn from the others who seem determined at all costs to prove them wrong, however long it may take to do so or however illogical their own argument can be shown to be.

A belief about God which arouses widespread derision concerns his existence 'outside' nature and consequent freedom from natural law. There is no way of proving this, say critics— and not only those who declare their own faith in science and for whom infinity can only denote a mathematical abstraction. But not all religious people believe in a God who is above question in this cognitive sense. To quote William James again:

> In the interest of Intellectual clearness, I feel bound
> to say that religious experience, as we have studied

it, cannot be cited as unequivocally supporting the infinitist belief (1929, 525).

Certainly developed theologies and religious systems give the impression of believing in a God who shares their rational approach and may be reached by argument; the more complex the theological structure, the less likely it is to be considered false, as human beings tend to be convinced by complexity and a system which includes infinity gives an impression of a God who is at least understandable. James goes on to point out that the only thing which his study establishes without any room for doubt is that we can experience union with *something* larger than ourselves and in that union find our greatest peace (1929, 525).

It seems then that that the Gods we worship do not need to be regarded as infinite in a theological sense. They simply have to be considered worthy of worship because of their comparative importance. They are greatly superior to us, but not necessarily in a metaphysical sense. Their divinity subsists in possessing more importance than anything else we know or can possibly imagine—not only because they can do more things than we can but because they can do them *better.* Thus their pre-eminence is not only quantitative but qualitative and our relationship to them strengthens us not only in what we are able to do but also, more importantly, what we able to be. To worship is a validating experience, establishing the worshipper in her or his own identity. You could say that from this point of view alone, without any metaphysical component at all, worship is self-justificatory.

It would be nearer the truth to say *theological* rather than metaphysical, however. Worship cannot avoid being a spiritual activity insofar as it involves reaching out towards what is not the self but is experienced as giving spiritual life to the self. The object of our worship is not like the self we carry about with us. It is sensed by us as another way of being which beckons to us from somewhere else and waits for us there. We ourselves also wait and, while we wait, we worship; for to worship is to want to draw nearer, to engage in a spiritual journey. Believers see this in terms of their belief in God; they know more about the road being travelled but they are not the only ones travelling along it.

The urge to worship seems stronger than the need to believe, that is, to have well-formulated religious beliefs concerning a God who is under no circumstances to be confused with oneself. Human spirituality reaches out and beyond the bounds of whatever it may be that we have already made part of ourselves to whatever remains 'unhomogenised.' It is this spiritual self, only existing as an absence, which gives rise to acts of worship. Worshippers are people who lack something precious and only the action of worshipping assuages their thirst for it.

I asked half-a dozen people to define spirituality for me:

> 'It's about the soul'
> 'Something beyond'
> 'A source of wholeness'
> 'Something to hope for'
> 'Trusting it's all worth while'
> 'When it's OK being you'
> 'Having faith when you can't prove anything'
> 'Going deeper'
> 'Going there. Being there'

I asked them to tell me more, and they did: spirituality, said the group, is belonging, accepting, blessing and being blessed; trusting, comfort, peace; depth, height. inwardness; something which sets me free and holds me safe; just not having to be anxious . . .

A small group, but many definitions, all of them different yet managing to say more or less the same thing without actually repeating themselves. One underlying theme was a sense of just being, picked up from an awareness of Being, present when anxiety has been displaced. Displaced by what? Nobody said.

Anxiety, says Heidegger (1996), is the emblem of our condition. It is the sign that we are authentically human. This doesn't apply to those who show obvious signs of it, the anxious people who manage to stand out in the crowd, but to all of us at some level or our awareness. Anxiety is what keeps us going, because it is the thing that keeps us searching. 'What's spiritually about? About coming home.' To the extent that they appear to be natural partners, spirituality is as much a human characteristic as anxiety.

Religion, however, is another matter. I didn't ask the group to define this for me, but I can imagine some of their answers: religion is about the Qur'an and Buddhist prayer wheels; nearer home, it concerns going to Mass and not playing in the garden on Sundays, having to try to believe impossible propositions, saying things by rote, finding ways of amusing yourselves during school assemblies. The test for religion would be as long as the one for spirituality. It would be quite different, however, although the subject of anxiety would figure here, too, implicitly if not explicitly.

In fact, religion depends on anxiety just as much as spirituality does. Without the conscious awareness of reasons for human beings to be anxious about their situation, and themselves within that situation, religion would not exist. The explicit nature of religious anxiety, and the answers to it which are offered, provide spiritual anxiety with a place of refuge, a home to return to, etc., and this is a function which explicit religion specifically performs for its members.

Not everything which seems religious describes itself as such. Commentators have drawn attention to various kinds of 'unofficial' religion, from 'folk religion' (i.e. traditions at odds with currently authorised religious belief), 'civic' or 'patriotic' religion' (largely consisting of the formal honouring of benefactors and those made heroic by the circumstances of their death 'for the nation'), and quite simply 'institutional' religion, or the sacredness associated with institutions *per se* as the embodiment of the aspiration of those who belong to them towards a kind of transpersonal significance which is able to exorcise individual anxieties. Georg Simmel (Frisby and Featherstone, 1997), writing over a century ago, speaks of 'the tragedy of culture,' by which he means the tendency of men and women to become servants of what they themselves have created—a kind of 'Frankenstein complex' operating on a species-characteristic scale promoting 'an ideal of sound life which functions as a quasi-religious basis, both for the present form of the institution and for successive transformations' (McFadyen, 1990, 241).

Such phenomena are usually considered to be non-doctrinal, and so they are in the usual sense of the word. However, they are all manifestations of the kind of special belonging in which individuals gain confidence as a result of seeing themselves as belonging within a particular social grouping, Tillich's 'courage to be as a part' (1962). This special belonging characterizes religious awareness and religions have often been regarded as systems contrived to regulate human interaction by addressing themselves, more of less directly, to the existential anxiety diagnosed by philosophers such as Heidegger, Binswanger and Sartre. Similarly those concerned with 'transpersonal' psychology (Grof, 1985; Washburn, 1994; Wilber, 1996) have described states of mind in which individual awareness is integrated with awareness which is shared and the anxiety of human vulnerability is transcended by 'the intuition of the single self.' The notion of separate existences becoming parts of an integrated whole is common to both religion and spirituality. Indeed, cognitive psychologists have regarded structure-building as a fundamental mechanism in the way human beings perceive themselves and the world they inhabit. George Kelly, for example, regards an individual's impulse to elaborate her or his own 'personal construct system' as the direct result of human vulnerability in the face of the unforeseeable:

> While it is events that one seeks to anticipate, one makes one's elaborative choice in order to define or extend the system which one has found useful in anticipating those events. We might call this 'a seeking of self protection' or 'acting in defence of the self' or 'the preservation of one's integrity' (Kelly, 1991, Vol. 1, 47).

Our aim in doing this is to arrive at a safe, or safer, way of relating to the unknown. Kelly regards systems primarily as ways of making sense. In order to do this, however, they must have something to make sense *of.* 'To us it seems meaningless to mention a system *qua system*. It must be a system for something.' As in *Gestalt* psychology things fall into place in order to make life capable of being lived. Making sense is what life is perceived to be *about.*

The suggestion here is that life is liveable to the extent that its circumstances are perceived as knowable. The ways in which this knowability is expressed and understood vary, however. Victor Frankl's 'logotherapy' (1977) regards explicitly religious belief as a way—*the* way in fact—of making sense of events. People whose spiritual awareness is less structured will draw comfort from a 'beyondness' which works for them in ways which are beyond words. There is a difference, however, between a more or less vague sense of the spiritual and the interpretation of religious significance according to a network of associated meanings each of them epistemologically satisfactory in terms of the whole—a story of life whose meaning is able to endorse the value of life for all who subscribe to it.

'If we are free to live our lives and to construct meanings for the phenomena around us as we choose, then we are responsible for ourselves.' So writes Fenella Quinn (2010, 43), describing her work to give disturbed children the 'emotional space to discover who they feel themselves to be.' Some of these children will choose to belong within a particular religion, some will not; all will have discovered the elusive appeal of spirituality whose fascination lies in its absence of structure, the beckoning vagueness of the outline it presents. We may search for some kind of pattern, a recognisable story, an argument to be fleshed out within the embodied experience of men and women, demonstrating its reality by its obvious presence in the world; but we will not find it here.

For some, the search is enough. It is better to travel than to arrive, these people say. Perhaps they have had experience of arriving in the wrong place and have resolved to abandon any kind of explicitly religious path towards spiritual fulfilment. Or perhaps the urge for making sense has led them merely to change tracks. The point is, however, that any move they decide to make will be in the direction of religion and away from spirituality—not necessarily *explicit* religion, however, because, as we shall see, there are other kinds of religious belonging. This fact is beginning to be more widely acknowledged than it has been in the past; it is hugely important for an understanding of the contemporary world. Psychologically speaking, the religious doctrines to which we hold fast are formed from our native capacity for spirituality which turns us in God's direction, away from ourselves, that is. Spiritual awareness allows God to draw us into his presence. Certainly it is a gift, something we did not invent ourselves— but, then, so is life. C. G. Jung certainly saw religious doctrine as emerging from the ocean of a shared spirituality; he described the way in which religious doctrines 'expressed aptly the living process of the unconscious in the form of repentance, sacrifice and redemption' (1938, 57). His 'collective unconscious' represents the totality of human spiritual awareness.

It would in fact be wrong for us to see religion and spirituality as in any way opposed to each other. If God's message is sent to us, we are equipped to receive it; the evidence of our own spirituality suggests that we are predisposed to do this. We ask ourselves and one another questions regarding purpose and value; we have strongly held views about the meaning of life, our own lives and human existence as a whole; we are fascinated by whatever resists our impulse to understand and control, searching for mysteries to go on exploring. All such questions are authentically spiritual, concerned with an aspect of our everyday experience which, owing to its identity as ordinary human behaviour, attracts little attention except to say that asking awkward questions is simply a part of being human.

During the last half century, however, the subject of spirituality as distinct from religion has come into the forefront of our thinking about the way we choose to answer this kind of question because, although it is rational for spirituality to endorse religion, it is equally reasonable for it to criticise it. As we saw, spirituality itself has no dogmatic framework; this means that religious systems which lay down rules about how life should be lived are open to criticism from those who choose to stay with a non-specific spirituality, as the rules of religion are regarded as restrictive simply by virtue of their being rules at all. The claim is frequently made that, since spirit is essentially free, we should strive not tie it down in any way but allow it to 'blow where it wills,' and try not to get in its way.

Spirit does not move aimlessly, however. Giving its own life to creatures, it goes on working through them. Spirit is active because it is purposeful, transforming both humanity and the things human beings make so that they too may be vehicles of spirit. Members of particular religions are conscious of God's Spirit at work in those ways, ceaselessly providing evidence of his presence, leaving his thumbprint on creation. The arrangements which religions make to establish their own discipleship and proclaim God in the world, because these things are inhabited by his presence, transmit his Spirit to any willing to receive it and make it welcome. Spirit, then, gives life to structure—the framework which holds things together for us—and structure is spirit; we communicate with God and one another through structures which at the individual and organisational level have lent themselves to acting as vehicles for spirit.

This, of course, is not to suggest that this is the only way in which spirit can act among us. As embodied love, spirit brings people together in relationship, the simplest human structure on which all other organisation is founded. Love is not the structure but, wherever it is made welcome by the structure, love abides. This may seen an obscure way of talking, more suitable for poetry, perhaps, that prose. These are subjects which, because they refuse to subject themselves to being used as objects of study, cannot be discussed in literal terms. For something as volatile and elusive as spirit, poetry is the only suitable language. Its aim is inscrutability so that we should not be distracted into concentrating on the messenger instead of the message. In poetry we search for the truth; the more obscure the language, the harder we search. Without undervaluing cognition, its usefulness for understanding religion is always limited. Knowledge of God is always spiritual, not something we have worked out for ourselves. It is something which we experience as a gift; we know this because, however hard we try to learn about a religion, we have no hope of really understanding it unless we are willing to let ourselves become involved in it—even if it goes no further than taking part in its ceremonies. Before it asks for our assent, religion calls for our conscious presence.

Spirituality, on the other hand, makes no demands but keeps on searching. A Zen Buddhist poem puts this well:

> The soul is a clear water, with gold fish and stars in it.
> By itself it does nothing.
> But if you chop wood it will light a fire
> If you build a boat it will become the ocean.

Religions are wood-choppers and boat-builders. From time to time they may lose track of which it is that they are doing, what it is that they are there to do. The soul's work of yearning for God opens them to the Spirit so that they may come to life again. Although they belong together, soul and spirit are not the same; like Yin and Yang, they complete each other, the first as question, the second as answer. Unlike the soul, spirit is not something which may be counted on or taken for granted which, of course, is why we talk of 'inspiration.'

> Rarely, rarely, comest thou,
> Spirit of Delight!
> . . .
> Thou art love and life! Oh come,
> Make once more my heart thy home (Shelley, 1917, 'Song' 633).

Shelley's poem is not intended to be religious in any formal sense. The poet knows his request is in vain but this will not stop him asking, and therein lies his salvation, in reaching out to the giver of inspiration. Overtly religious people may well feel this is a little vague but this may be simply because spirit addresses them in a different way as is bound to happen when the source of their delight is identified as divine and spirit becomes Spirit. All the same, it is not only actual divinity which attracts worship; on the contrary, our devotion is given to whatever invites us to participate in something which we recognise as infinitely greater and more worthwhile than anything else—including any specifically religious teaching we have received in the past.

Spirituality does not summon to worship but religion does. The object of actual worship must be identified so that we know who or what it is that calls us to bow down to the super-ordinance that we perceive. Spirituality, on the other hand, our own spirituality, draws to the object of our devotion, infusing it with its own mysterious quality. When this happens, whatever our own soul aspires towards is given a spurious numinosity, a holiness which is actually the reflection of our own spiritual yearning. To this extend, Feuerbach was justified in his claim that religion may be understood as 'nothing else than the consciousness which man has of his own—not finite and limited but infinite—nature' (Bettis, 1969, 116). In fact, Feuerbach overreaches himself; it is not religion which may double back on itself in this way but the human spiritual urge to worship transcendence even if it is disposed to create it for itself. In other words, to do what Feuerbach wrongly accused religious people of doing—which is to make God in their own image.

This is the danger implicit in spirituality that, in its eagerness to find a god to worship, we may easily choose someone or something which we know very well is not intrinsically divine and endue them or it with our own sense of the spiritual. Such is the human need to worship that this may in some circumstances be an easy thing to do. We shall be returning to this later but, for the time being, it is enough to say that if, for reasons of human social circumstance and individual experience, the God who is really God seems hard to contact, or even not worth contacting, then human beings are both willing and able to put up with substitutes.

CHAPTER 4

Therefore, my dear friends, flee from the worship of
idols (1 Cor 10:14).

G. K. Chesterton is usually credited with the remark that,
'When men stop believing in God, they don't believe in nothing;
they believe in anything.' Whether or not it was Chesterton
himself who said this—or perhaps even Father Brown who said
something very like it[1]—there seems little doubt that it accords
with the facts. It is exceedingly common for people to worship
whatever they are emotionally involved with and regard as
essentially of greater worth than they are themselves. Such an
attitude fits the dictionary definition of 'worship' as 'adoration or
devotion' (McIntosh, 1964, 1508) but scarcely constitutes religious
experience even when it awakens feelings of spirituality. We feel
'as if' the thing or person were divine even while knowing that it
or they are not. We are in the area of poetry and metaphor rather
than religious belief which, again referring to the dictionary, is
'acceptance of any received theology.' Within the spiritual sphere,
however, metaphor acts in the same way as doctrine does in
religion, as a way of identifying ideas and feelings perceived as
hard to grasp and yet critically important: soul-messages.

Worship and belief belong together; so do worship and religious doctrine, the 'teaching of the story,' but not quite so closely. Historians of religion have tended to see actual teaching about God as having emerged from sacerdotal practices of various kinds, corporate ritual in particular, which would involve instruction regarding the necessity to carry out acts of worship along with training in how to do this in the approved way (Grainger, 1974). There would, however, have been no mandatory verbal or written account of the actions and identity of the one who was to be worshipped, only that this was a god perceived as taking account of human beings and their needs and as such could be cajoled or placated but never actually controlled.

Suppositions such as these, however difficult to substantiate from the viewpoint of historical scholarship, lend support to the idea that religion and worship are very closely allied, so closely in fact as to be inseparable in a way that arguments concerning religious truth, and religion itself, are not. For all practical purposes worship and religious belief are identical, so that we worship what we believe in and believe in what we worship. On reflection, this is not as surprising as it seems, considering the interchange of guest and host according to which, as we have seen, each reaches out to the other and our human soul reaches out to receive the Spirit which searches for it, refusing to rest until it has been found: until each of them has found the other.

The action of worshipping, then, is a fundamentally human gesture, whereas acceptance of religious propositions is not, although the freedom to accept or reflect them certainly is. If there are things which happen to us in our lives—experiences or ideas which have aroused a sense of their unique and overriding importance for us, we may very well end up worshipping them. The act of doing this will give us joy and satisfaction because of the spirit we ourselves have bestowed on them which reflects back on us in a way which makes us less anxious. Even if we knew very well that what we are adoring in such as way is really not worthy of our devotion, the act of regarding it as if it were makes us participators in the holiness which we ourselves have given it. In this way, Dr Faustus in Christopher Marlowe's play gazes at the objects of desire and says, 'This feeds my soul' (Marlowe, 1609, Sc. VI).

Faustus was well aware of committing blasphemy but those who worship what they love and admire because they themselves have made it worthy of devotion do not necessarily feel that they are behaving in a religious way and would be affronted by the suggestion that this is what they are in fact doing. What really matters here, however, is the quality of the devotion offered. Religious devotion is a unique commitment of the soul, not to be confused with other kinds of human attachment, however intense; in other words, we sense it as *qualitatively* different from human loving. This is true even though we may be spiritually enriched by the love we have for another. In Tennyson's *Idylls of the King* Queen Guinevere grieves that she has allowed her love for Lancelot to distract her from her devotion to God, declaring that, 'We must love the highest when we see it' (Tennyson, 1921, *Idylls of the King*; l. 651). These are the words of a passionate woman rather than of a nun.

It hardly needs saying that we can be spiritually moved by other experiences than that of coming into the presence of God. Spirit speaks to us though our own spirituality, moving between and among us and encouraging us to inspire, and to be inspired by, others. Martin Buber describes how we communicate spiritually with one another by the way we use impersonal objects in order to make them personal:

> This is the eternal source of art; a man is faced by
> form which desires to be made through him into a
> work . . . The man is concerned with an act of his
> being. If he carries it through, then the effective
> power streams out and the work arises (Buber, 1958,
> 9, 10).

In other words, our 'effective power' is another way of describing how our soul causes objects and ideas to become the media for spiritual communication between individuals. To put it more crudely, a work of art is a human spirit enshrined in concrete form for the purpose of 'inspiring and blessing.' Buber says clearly that the artwork, whatever it may be, is not the product of a human soul but its vehicle. As such it is capable of arousing recognition from other souls. However, although we are inspired by works of art, we should not worship them—the spirit which they embody is a human one like our own. This is something which cannot ever be over-stressed for the relationship between our human spirit and the divine spirit of God is the subject of all true worship. It is this relationship which religion itself formalises within our minds and embodies in our actions. It is emphatically not something we have made for ourselves.

In religious terms, to worship what one has made oneself— and *for* oneself—constitutes idolatry. This is not so, of course, for those who see themselves as non-religious. How could it be? To commit an offence against someone you don't believe exists is obviously nonsense; to commit it against an existence you yourself have invented by setting out to enliven it through your own native spirituality makes more sense because of the obvious debt which something like that owes its creator. Psychologists have underlined the normality of such behaviour among the children they have studied, as toys are brought to life so that the joys and agonies, victories and defeats of life can be played out at their expense without anybody being really hurt: that is, anybody *real.* The child savours the experience of being in control instead of being ineffective or even, on some occasions, totally impotent. D. W. Winnicott describes how a doll is transformed into a Mother who can now survive having her head banged, oh so brutally, against the window frame.

To this extent, all idols serve as 'transitional objects,' preparing the way for something not yet accomplished, an unfulfilled wholeness. In Winnicott's words, 'incomplete adaptation to need makes objects real' (1971, 10, 11). At this stage of development a child's awareness of other people, particularly its mother, as realistically other, a separate person in fact, is far from well established. The transitional object functions in order to bridge the gap between the other and the self by being given a life of its own, one which is separate and therefore able to move in either direction. 'The transitional object is never under magical control like the internal object, not is it outside control as the real mother is' (1971, 10).

Separate, but certainly not independent. Although the transitional object possesses the ability to stand in for the mother, it owes its 'life' to having been charged with the child's creative imagination without which life in the real world of people and things would be forever out of its reach. It is as if the child were saying:

> 'This doll, teddy bear, comfort blanket is, to me, both safety and adventure. It can be whatever I want to make it and do anything I want it to do. If I have any kind of problem, it can help me with it. The

only thing I cannot do with it is make it vanish. But
that's how I know it is real.'

The kind of creative imagining which Winnicott describes
seems hard to distinguish from the search for engagement which
we have been considering. Both imagination and spirituality
represent the human need to reach beyond the self as in the
first place we ourselves reached out to the source of our life.
Whether we address the person concerned as father or mother,
they are known to be essential to our peace and so we make the
effort to try to perpetuate their presence by using whatever the
environment can offer as a symbol.

It is not only infants who do this. Winnicott is quite clear
about this. Indeed the process he describes is so formative of
human development, so fundamental to the way we become
persons at all, that it cannot simply be dismissed as a phase
children pass through; after all, we do not go on playing with
teddy bears for very long. We do, however, continue to play with
other things, some of which do very much the same job for us.
This is what Winnicott himself has to say:

> The thing about playing is always the precariousness
> of the interplay of personal psychic reality and the
> experience of control of actual objects. This is the
> precariousness of magic itself that arises in intimacy,
> in a relationship that is being found to be reliable
> (1971, 47).

Hence the satisfaction attached to ideas that can be 'played
around with,' presences that can be invoked and dismissed at
will, which feeds our urge to express ourselves in useful objects

and works of art, systems and projects, organisational structures and holiday plans. Playing influences all our seriousness because it represents a creative condition of in-betweenness, something which is at once unreal and yet real.

Winnicott refers to this as 'magic,' probably because he can find no other word for it in the medical dictionary. Its precariousness is confined to the business of trying to define it as in fact it is genuinely functional and extremely practical. Our minds refuse to work properly without it. Playing is essential for the achievement of every kind of human purpose, whether utterly serious or entirely trivial, that is, changing a light bulb or worshipping God. Theologically speaking, organised worship is playing, proclaiming our inability to do something in the way it ought to be done. If we imagine that it is being done properly—that *we* are doing it properly—we find ourselves drawn into worshipping it for itself rather than for what it means, worshipping the messenger rather than the message. It is very easy for us to worship the things we have made ourselves because we ourselves are able to control them. We can use them well or badly, for good or evil. We have given them a dependent life, one derived from our own, which is easy enough to imagine is now theirs rather than ours. It has to be, so that they can be persuaded to reflect back on us and we may feel we are receiving as well as just giving. This is the relationship we have with our toys and we find no difficulty in imagining it to be personal.

It does not have to be an intense relationship, of course, because it is after all only a game. How much of ourselves we receive from it and give to it depends on how necessary we feel it is to us, the role it plays in the satisfaction we are able to derive from life. If it plays a critical role for us, we come to rank it higher than anything else in our personal scale of values. The more we invest ourselves in in it, the more it becomes the symbol of all excellence, transforming the ordinariness of our lives through our association with it. The yearning for spiritual fulfilment, which is the human aptitude for worship, finds satisfaction in exalting what has been artificially raised to the condition of the divine in order to pay it the homage it is perceived as deserving. Whatever it was or is, this thing was far from being a god until someone made it into one for themselves.

It hardly needs pointing out that, from a religious angle, this constitutes idolatry. We should not attempt to create gods because we already have one of our own. From the point of view of religion, the notion of a man-made god is nonsensical. Because it is such an easy thing to manufacture one's own gods, it appears to religious people to be extremely dangerous—which is why the world's sacred texts abound in warnings against it.[2] To worship an image as if it were God is to render oneself ineligible for knowing God himself. In the circumstances it is the worst way of insulting him. The Jewish prophets saw it as both foolish and wicked:

> The idols of the nations are silver and gold, the work
> of human hands.
> They have mouths, but they do not speak; they have
> eyes, but they do not see; they have ears, but they do
> not hear, and there is no breath in their mouths.
> Those who make them become like them, . . .
> (Ps 135:15-18).

Thus says the Psalmist and idolatry is a dominant theme in the rest of the bible, being mentioned almost seventy times in the Old Testament, as well as eleven in the New Testament. 'Little children, keep yourselves from idols,' warns St John (1 Jn 5:21), in the same way that Paul, in his first letter to the Corinthian Christians, reminds them very firmly of the dangers of indulging in practices traditionally regarded as idolatrous:

> . . . we know that "no idol in the world really exists," and that "there is no God but one." Indeed even though there may be so-called gods in heaven or on earth—as in fact there are many gods and many lords—yet for us there is one God, the Father, from whom are all things and for whom we exist, and one Lord, Jesus Christ, through whom are all things and through whom we exist (1 Cor 8:4-6).

God's living presence reveals all rival deities as essentially self-made. There can never be any comparison, that is, if you are religiously inclined, believing that God has called you to him in some way. The thrust of this book, however, is directed towards those who would hesitate to say that the object of their devotion was divine—divinity not being a category they are willing to recognise. It may be that these people are like St Paul's Athenians (Ac:17:22ff) who are unaware who it is that they are actually worshipping and have created their own substitute, generated from their own spirituality in order to satisfy a worship-hunger which is also their own.

We should recognise, however, that, considering what we have been saying earlier about the human spirit's restlessness, we must be careful before judging this behaviour too harshly. If it is a sin, it is also a fundamental characteristic of the species to which we belong. Those who see themselves as having found—or having been found by—the Spirit of God are extremely blessed and part of their blessedness is the joy of serving as a reminder to those who interpret life differently that they would benefit from keeping an open mind regarding the possibility of a deeper satisfaction, a more profound joyfulness, than they receive from whatever deity they are already engaged in worshipping. If there was ever a time when to worship him was accepted as the most attractive option offered by God to his world, that time is certainly long past. We accept the many gifts he offers us but not necessarily the gift of himself. There are many cultural reasons why this is so and much has been written about them. This book offers the theological reason that God's image and likeness is shown in our personal need to share the life of spirit in whatever way we feel we can. There are endless opportunities for doing this with our fellow women and men and, when for cultural reasons we lose our inclination to set any store by the god-hypothesis, we are both able and willing to make do with a substitute.

It is easy for religious people to underestimate the significance of the networks of meanings and values which we ourselves construct in order to communicate with one another, drawing conclusions from the similarities and differences which occur among them. In the business of making sense of the world the latter are as important as the former, the most crucial being the distinction we make between the things we and other people have brought into being, by this process of putting together and keeping separate, and whatever has been organised without our aid. Claude Lévi-Strauss (1970) refers to this distinction as the difference between 'culture'—the things we have made—and 'nature'—whatever it may be that we have used in order to make them. Religious thought recognises God as the original craftsman while discriminating between vessel and potter. It recognises, however, that, for the purpose of creating a world, both are necessary.

As the work of the creative spirit which we enjoy by virtue of our humanity, culture is able to wield considerable authority over the way we perceive the world we live in. As the social philosopher Georg Simmel maintained (Frisby and Featherstone, 1997), the tragedy of human culture belongs to the fact that, although we ourselves create it, we are totally dominated by whatever it is that we are imposing on ourselves by doing so. It is as if societies, by virtue of their being human constructions, exist in the grip of a 'Frankenstein complex' from which they are not able to free themselves! This may seem over-dramatic but, when we reflect on the way that scientific culture has taken over vast areas of the globe during the last few centuries, so that no other explanation of reality bears the stamp of social acceptance and every other epistemological position is reduced to the level of a minority interest, we may perhaps begin to realise why spirituality has been diverted into alternative ways of expressing itself. In the next chapter, we shall be looking at some of these.

CHAPTER 5

The biblical prohibition of idolatry mainly concerns the behaviour of groups of people and centres on the abuse of corporate worship. It is this interpersonal aspect of religious behaviour which attracts the attention of sociologists. For example, Émile Durkheim (1915) was particularly interested in the emotional sharing involved in corporate ritual which he saw as the origin of religion itself. Others have seen the practice of public religion as a way of legitimising the arrangements made by society to regulate its affairs. Max Weber (1965), however, tended to see this happening in reverse, painting to a concordance between religious practice and social structure according to which the ways different societies are constructed reveal the kinds of religion they are likely to have. If a particular religion is dominant within a social structure, this itself is an indication of the way in which the fundamental difference between the sacred and the profane is understood. For him, religious awareness, shown by the social significance of religious practices, was as important as it was later for Lévi-Strauss (1970).

'A person will worship something, have no doubt about that.' So says Emerson in Essay 17 'Worship' (1910). It seems that, even in the secularist atmosphere of the twenty-first century, this saying still holds true. The sociology of religion is in debt to Edward

Bailey's suggestion (1997) that contemporary culture actually makes room for two kinds of religion, which he calls 'explicit' and 'implicit.' Sociologically speaking, the second kind of religious belonging functions as the first does without actually calling itself a religion at all. Nevertheless, it gives rise to the same kind of behaviour as religion does and also to an identical quality of personal experience. Anything which is 'implicitly' religious but not 'explicitly' so complies with three particular requirements, the first of them being the ability to induce commitment in those associated with it. In other words, it must carry with it a high degree of devotedness which acts as validation of someone's personal identity. Commitment is expressed by resolution to remain faithful to a certain way of feeling and thinking. It is associated with belief in the central importance and value of something and the determination to behave in accordance with this belief. Bailey's second defining characteristic of the phenomenon he is describing is what he calls 'integrating foci.' In other words, commitments bring with them an intensified awareness of what it is that inspires them so that everything else which concerns individuals draws its own meaning and significance from the importance and value of whatever it is that is a person's primary focus.

Definition number three completes the picture by widening it out and highlighting its sociological function. Religion identified as implicit is a way of thinking, feeling and behaviour which, as well as concentrating individual experiences, lays claim to a widening horizon of awareness, and this functions as 'intensive concerns with extensive effects.' Implicit religion refers to a fact of human experience able to change the way we see the world around ourselves so that mere comprehensive perception may lead to increased involvement in social action. Like Bailey's other two definitions, this is not intended as final and exclusive, the aim always being to draw closer to something which is intrinsically hard to pin down but, at the same time, known to be a real part of human experiences. This is why definitions of implicit religion continue to emerge. From a sociological point of view these three phenomenological hallmarks add up to a credible description of religious behaviour, in spite of the fact that those who see life through these spectacles do not need to consider themselves to be religious at all; in other words, they do not necessarily belong to any social grouping whose members subscribe to anything that is generally thought of as a religion.

More than twenty four years of investigating areas of social activity which might be expected to produce examples of action which could be classed as implicitly religious have shown how extremely widespread such behaviour is. In fact, the tendency would appear to be perfectly normal. People are attached to sport, food and drink, art and science, social prestige (all kinds of clubs, professional, commercial, political), trade unions, professions, 'movements,' public and private idealisms, wealth and possessions, fame and success, notoriety—all these and many more are eligible to become, for us, the only thing which makes life worth living. We are not talking here of being interested in, or attracted, by these things but of treating them as essentially more valuable than anything else could ever be, in other words, worshipping them.

It would be extremely easy for people who know themselves to be religious (according to the usual understanding of the word) to acknowledge the spirituality of this kind of attachment. The truth is, however, that, as we have seen, those who worship these things invest their own spirituality in them. This is the spirituality which is native to human beings as children of God. The image of God the Father lives in the exchange of joy. In the thought of

'Abdu'l-Bahá, the universe is an overflowing of divine bounty whose purpose is precisely this, the creation of joy among human beings:

Is any larger bounty conceivable than this, that an individual, looking within himself, should find that by the confirming grace of God he has become the cause of peace and well-being, of happiness and advantage to his fellow men? (1990, 116)

If indeed we are created in the image and likeness of God (Gen 1:27), the effect lies in our ability to exchange love. God regards us a love-bearers. We may, of course, abuse this capacity for loving and we do this by turning away from one another or, more strictly, from God-in-one-another and one-another-in-God. If we use the freedom of love by focusing it solely upon ourselves, we deprive it of life; however, the capacity to love abides in us so that we remain capable of using it the way we were meant to do. Such is the image which God has of us through his presence among us.

Our image of him, on the other hand, is likely to take several forms. It can be:

> *personal* God who brings us into enabling contact with himself
> *distant* God who is there but cannot be reached by us or evades our attempts to contact him
> *abstract* God who is the answer to theoretical problems and whose existence explains things
> *irrelevant* God exists (perhaps) but this has no bearing on our lives and the business of living them
> *absent* God does not exist; so there isn't any point in our thinking about him

punitive God who is waiting to punish us; God as
Nemesis
taboo God who is dangerous to think about; the God
of neurotic symptomology (Dawkins, 2007)
unintelligible the God who can only be believed in
by others
impersonal the force which causes things to happen
surprising God who keeps reminding us of who he
is—and what he is like—when we have forgotten.

These are just ten of the ways in which God is thought about.
There are obviously more than these. In a sense, there are as many
ways as there are people who imagine him. Some of the things
listed above make conscious contact with his image difficult
or perhaps impossible; no-one can really relate to absence of
credibility and opacity, aversive or punitive intent, capriciousness
or ruthless impersonality. If these are the ways in which people
picture God, it is not surprising if they prefer to think of other
things instead. The absence of a firm conviction that God and
love are inseparable leaves room for other ideas about his identity,
to the extent of refusing to believe that he actually has one—
for hasn't science made thinking about God unnecessary? Being
unable to believe in him does not cancel his gift of love, however;
nor does it take away the need to find ways to exercise that gift.

Whether we think or refuse to think about God, we appear
to be unable to stop searching for ways to find him. These may be
either explicit or implicit, conscious or unconscious, well-hidden
or exposed to view. The searching itself is not hidden, only the
route which it takes; nor is the love which inspires the search
because we receive back everything we invest. This continues
to be the case for as long as we go on investing; when we stop

loving, then the love we feel ourselves receiving stops too, so that it becomes necessary to find another outlet for it. As we have seen, such loving is a necessity for the human spirit so that not to love at all is a kind of emotional suicide. What we love can be almost anything but is most likely to be a person or a group of people or a movement involving people. It is a transferable kind of loving and, as spirit, it settles on those who feel they will benefit from its presence and from the opportunity of running with it. However, it has to be mutual, or at least perceived as such; otherwise it will soon fade and start to decay.

People who belong to a religion know that God's love is not like this. They know that he does not stop loving us even when we stop loving him. For one thing, having created us, he 'knoweth wherof we are made' (Ps 103:14); he is aware that it may be necessary for such things to happen so that his love may be re-discovered. He has both embodied us and imbued us with the spiritual capacity to exchange love for, by living in his image, we bear personal responsibility for choosing where and with whom to exchange it. It is precisely this absence of focus which is the most pronounced characteristic of our spirituality. Because of its vagueness from the point of view of actual definition—some might say its blessed vagueness—we are able to invoke it to illuminate areas of our experience which have transpersonal significance and consequently resist being embodied in scientific language of any kind. This allows us to talk about God and his relationship with us without even knowing that that is what we are doing.

This accounts for the way in which things which are not religious, in the sense of being involved in worshipping God, may still be used as the objects of devotion; for whether religion is explicit or not, it must always involve spirituality through its ability to evoke a spiritual responsiveness in us. Whether the love around in our hearts is love exchanged with God or with something or someone else that we love, it remains a loving, thankful gesture on our part, the movement of the self away from itself towards the other, and therefore something acceptable to God, although not intentionally offered to him.

Nor, however, is it intentionally denied him. The children of Israel who, in time of stress, turned away from Yahweh in order to worship gods which they had made for themselves may be supposed to have known very well what it was they were doing. If they had not known and had abstained from pledging themselves to following Moses' leadership, their offence would not have been so great. In a sense, it may not actually have been an offence at all. We do not deliberately turn away from God in order to serve what we ourselves acknowledge as a mere substitute for him, a lifeless object on which it would be pointless to think of depending for any kind of help. What it is that we have put together must be brought to life before it can really be of any use at all. The way in which we do this is by the gift of our own human spirit and allowing that to reflect back on ourselves. The fact that what we have made lacks its own independent life is less harmful to our relationship with God than the action of deliberately setting out to find a substitute for him.

In the bible, then, idolatry is a personal affront to God. This is not the case with worship which reproduces behaviour associated with religious belonging without regarding itself as religious in the sense of believing in God. From a human point of view, idolatry is a sin committed against the God in whom one believes! Implicit religion does not deny god so much as leave him out of the equation. Because of this it differs fundamentally from idolatry. Religious people's own experience continues to remind them how easy it is to regard human beings themselves and the arrangements they make for living as the most precious thing in life so that they usurp the position which should rightfully be acknowledged as belonging only to God. This is something we all tend to do without knowing we are doing it although putting God first in no way undervalues things which he has made. Quite the opposite in fact, those who love God love what he has given them to be loved on his behalf.

This act of human loving does not necessarily depend on understanding in the sense of believing that such-and-such is the case. It has more to do with surrender than comprehension; we relinquish the freedom to keep someone or something at a distance. In other words, we *trust* whoever or whatever it may be enough to put ourselves in danger of being rejected. In love, abandoning our autonomy is a release rather than a restriction. This is something to do with the condition of loving rather than the actual object of love, however. Thus, whether we abandon our defensiveness for God or someone or something else, we are spiritually restored by our loving. If we believe in God, we recognise his work in what is happening to us; if, for some reason, we are unable or unwilling to do such a thing, then we rejoice and are blessed by God who is himself love.

If we believe in God, that is. Fewer actually claim to do this than formerly. This is dramatically the case in western Europe, even among those who say they believe but abstain from attending worship. Students of implicit religion point out that official—that is, explicit—religion is in process of being slowly edged out of its former position by religious belonging of a kind which is not explicitly God-centred. There is certainly a great deal of evidence that this is actually happening, as commercial advertising on television and at the roadside extols its products in language formerly reserved for religion and football teams wave the banner of 'Power! Passion! Belief!' leaving their supporters in no doubt at all as to who it is they are being urged to believe in.

Supporters or worshippers? Implicit religion has little doubt that both descriptions are accurate. What it has to say, however, is more positive than simply to deplore secularism and indulge in nostalgia for times when people were more discriminating about what they worshipped. This disguised and diverted species of devotion should be seen for what it, in fact, is: the expression of 'a dimension of human being' (Bailey, 2001, 44). We have seen how spirituality, our own yearning for human fulfilment, leads us to make gods of what we perceive around us. Bailey reminds us that this same spirituality is 'the form taken by religiosity in contemporary culture.' Religious awareness, he says, has now shifted its focus from a culturally discredited deity to what he calls 'a commitment to be human' (2001, 81).

All the same, there is a difference between religious feeling which is now directed humanwards and religious thinking which is bound to be handicapped by the prosaic nature, the sheer familiarity of its new object. Spirituality does not simply search for a host; it reaches out for divinity, bestowing transcendence on whatever arouses its devotion. There are those who will continue to worship God as God and, for them, to engage in implicit religion will appear as a kind of contemporary idolatry.

CHAPTER 6

Happy are those who live in your house, ever singing
your praises (Ps 84:4).

Can any spirituality not centred upon the God of developed
doctrinal construction actually be taken as authentically religious?
These who belong to religions which set out to identify themselves
as such would almost certainly say such a thing would be
impossible, involving a contradiction in terms. Religious belief,
they would argue, actually means taking account of a Being
understood as categorically other than mankind: someone, or
something, imagined in terms of distance, beyondness, reachable
only on their own terms which involve the willingness to become
a member of a particular religion. Belief is identical with the
acceptance of specific doctrines and denial of all other approaches.
Because we are rational creatures, we are required to give assent
to whatever is involved in joining at an intellectual level. In a
way, this is reasonable enough because religions hold together
because of the willingness of their members to hold to a particular
interpretation of reality.

At the same time it takes more to become a convert than
the conscious decision to start seeing things according to
the rules binding upon the members of a particular religion.

Experience shows that religious belonging has more to do with intense personal experiences than reasoned arguments about the credibility of specific beliefs. Argument may follow spiritual awakening, as it did so strikingly with St Paul, but it is the transforming event in our own life which opens up the heaven for us. In fact, genuine religion, although it tries to give an account for itself in terms of ideas and arguments, is really more to do with feelings than thoughts—the evidence of passion forged on so many separate Damascus roads. Perhaps thoughts, doctrines, sets of interconnected religious ideas, are needed to hold emotions together and keep them safely contained.

Unfortunately, spiritually awakened people react against being told precisely how to interpret what has happened to them. Perhaps they set less store by having to give intellectual assent to other people's interpretations of events whose significance is uniquely their own. They don't wish to be told what to believe and how to believe it. This is not because they question the credibility of the account put before them but because their own religious experience resists the regularisation involved in intellectual acceptance of religious formulae. Their own experience may have been far less dramatic than the apostle's; indeed, it could have consisted of a gradual unfolding of spiritual awareness without any startling episodes; whatever form it took, however, it was something deep enough to have changed a life. As William James (1929) says, this may happen in many ways. For example, someone may say that they whole-heartedly believe in God, only they find it impossible to do so in the way religion requires that they should. If asked to be more precise, they would go on to say that they believed that human beings always managed to connect with God in some way or other but that there were different approaches, some of them more religious than others. They might even point out that the religion to which they themselves belonged was strict in its teaching and strongly resisted all views but its own. I can't live with a religion which never allows you to disagree, they would say.

At this point it is worth summarising what was said earlier about religions which concentrate on telling stories, as most do. Human beings are led not only by their thoughts and feelings but by their capacity for spiritual awareness. In a social setting in which organised religion is tolerated but largely discounted an individual is put in a position where she or he must choose carefully in which direction to turn in order to enjoy his or her sense of spiritual fulfilment. Some organised religions choose to instruct their members to direct their native spirituality along well-defined lines, working on the principle that intellectual understanding of the story's message is the best way of doing this. This in itself is a reasonable approach, as anybody who reflects on the way that the story of someone else's experience tunes in with experiences of our own will readily agree. Story arouses feelings and feelings give rise to thoughts.

In that order: observation, feeling, thought. Why, we observe in the first place, is because of a spiritual link between ourselves and others, which is the origin of all story-telling whatever the story may be about. Thus it is always possible for this approach to work against itself, particularly in circumstances in which the social value of religion is denied and its personal significance largely discounted. The general opinion, at least in western Europe, is that religion is an essentially private affair, organised religion being seen as associations of like-minded people. This, too, would appear to be the attitude of religions themselves, who have traditionally related like-mindedness higher than anything else. Nowadays, however, people, even some who regard themselves as religious, may tend to disagree.

Admittedly, when our own view is corroborated by everyone else who is around, we do feel somewhat comforted. If everybody agrees that something is true, then that is more or less the same as its being true. The mind is comfortable with similarities and thinks round things in order to get them to add up. Actual understanding, however, does not depend just on thinking in a detached, disembodied way and, even when thought carries with it an emotional charge, it takes more than this to convince us that something is really happening to us and our world—and, when we do become aware, it is the awareness itself which acts upon us. Actual experience is that which comes to us and stays with us. It is this that registers with us, not simply our thoughts about it.

Understanding, then, is our whole experience of something and we are affected more by the existential than the theoretical. So much is obvious, perhaps. What is not so obvious is that it is kinetic rather than static; in other words, we carry it around with us. What we understand is always in a particular setting either among other people or absent from them, so that it is not only ideas which are contextual but also objects, human or otherwise, present or past; for it is precisely the memory of their being there which comes home to us, not as an idea but as an actual physical presence. It is the experience of being in a particular place along with whomever and whatever is there with you at that specific moment, speaking and being spoken to, touching and being touched, either communicating with them or feeling cut off from them. Human understanding is about moving in space shared with others and the reality of actual experience, its this-ness, here-ness and how-ness; it is sensory awareness which lives according to Eugene Gendlin (1981, 78) 'in the middle of our body.' Understanding, then, is what we sense. How can it be otherwise when each of us is an embodied presence?

If sharing thought creates barriers, laying down rules as to who is qualified to belong to a particular group of religious people and who ought to be excluded fro it, we may still relate via our embodied senses, through the tenderness which is the incarnate Love that is God. Elizabeth Baxter assures us that 'Conflicts in the churches arise from disembodied ways of theologizing' (2013). She is referring to conflicts existing within a religion but what she is saying applies equally well to the differences between them. A wholly intellectual definition of human understanding instructs us to imagine that only thinking, *working things out*, has any real significance so far as theological truth is concerned and relies on our ability to draw conclusions which can then be handed over to others for them to think about. Religion is about communicated thought rather than sensed experience.

The result is that the bodily dimensions of human awareness may be seen as hampering religion and only cognition is capable of receiving and responding to the messages which God sends. It is as if, of the four 'psychic functions' recognised by Jung as characterising the working of the human mind, namely, cognition, affect, sensation and intuition, only the first is genuinely capable of being in communion with God. If this is so, then the rest are dangerous distractions, 'sins of the the flesh,' in fact. Nevertheless, the experience of religious people themselves attests to the fact that the person whose faith is strongest is unlikely to be the one with the formal intellectual grasp of the definitive teachings of his or her religion but the one who has given their heart to it. The most accurate definition of religious belief, then, would be understanding with the heart. This is a spiritual quality which is expressed in the way we relate to other people, what it is that lies between and among us. The things which we read and hear about our faith and what we tell one another about it must be translated into things which affect the quality of people's lives: what it feels like to be alive.

'Religion represents life at its most intense.' Edward Bailey quotes Stanley Cook, writing as long ago as 1918. For Bailey, genuine religion as formerly understood has shifted its focus. The passing of time has only served to confirm Cook's verdict as, in contemporary culture, 'consciousness becomes both highly conscious of itself and of its context and the holy is diffused, . . . this time mainly at the human level' (Cook in Hastings et al., 1926, 662-693; Bailey, 2001). Religion's main task, therefore, is to represent itself as *part of life* in a way which makes sense nowadays, which means that the value of the spirituality characterising human experience everywhere, and not only in well-defined belief systems, should be acknowledged in the form it now takes as a positive affirmation of the worth of individuals and communities. Not only must God be proclaimed through organised religion but in other ways, too, by means of the spirituality which religious people have for so long been directed to discount and very often actually disparage.

Where loves rules, its presence should not be denied for intellectual reasons or indeed for any reasons. We must learn to recognise God in other places than among his conscious worshippers. We must learn to praise him through what we personally see and hear around us instead of seeking to take shelter from those whose idea of God differs from ours or who simply have no idea of him at all. We must look more closely at the way in which they live in the world and the love which is shown by their attitude to the lives of other people, aware how this reflects the glory of God, whether or not this is an idea which makes any sense to them. We must learn to let God be God and not be so taken up with what concerns our own success, or lack of it. Instead we must open our eyes to what it is that we ourselves are hearing and seeing around us: blind people receiving their sight, lame people walking again, lepers—of various kinds— being received back into society along with all the other benefits of Christ's unacknowledged presence in the world (Mt 11:4).

All these are evidence of love's persistence. Organised religion claims to be aware of this but is currently too taken up with examining its own credentials to appear to take the message as seriously as it should. The message of peace may be proclaimed but not to everyone, only those who speak special religious languages and have been carefully instructed to think in special religious ways. Peace and joy are offered but not to those who, as human beings, simply belong to God but only to those who belong to particular religions and can be regarded as safe because they are in possession of its rules. Perhaps it has always been like this and religion and group membership are, as Durkheim claimed, simply varying intensities of the same phenomenon's strengths. If this is true, then so far as its message about a love which is all-consuming, all-embracing, goes, organised religion has proved to be its own worst enemy through its determination to persevere in rescuing people from the world in order to include them in its own ranks. Group membership is certainly a means of support and reassurance but groups themselves divide society just as much as they unite it, particularly groups which have become exclusive by losing contact with the rest of society. Even if a group uses a special language to express its uniqueness, it still must be one which is intelligible to outsiders with whom it wishes to communicate with a view to including them in its own world-view; it must be part of a common tongue or the message will fail to be delivered. Within our society this language no longer exists, forcing such groups to talk more and more exclusively with their own kind.

This is not only so within the religious sphere, of course. As people grow increasingly technological in their thinking, their interest shifts further away from areas which appear alien to any approach other than the scientific, not science itself but a particular application of science to a particular problem which can only be solved by some kind of technical skill. Professional scientists already speak to one another in languages which neither non-professionals nor members of other professions are likely to be able to understand, although they may be envious of those who are fortunate enough to do so. Some of those who 'know the jargon' may themselves belong to a particular religion—religion being willing to include science in its thinking even though science is unable to reciprocate—but, generally speaking, spiritual things are generally assumed to have nothing to say of any actual importance to a society whose creed could be described as 'implicit materialism.' Thus the entire realm of spiritual reality has been deleted from the account of our lives which we officially formulate for ourselves.

Religion has a different account of itself but no language in which to give it, none, that is, which will be understood in terms of the dominant world-view within our society. This does not mean that religious people are forced to abandon their ways of thinking and talking about the experiences which, for them, proclaim the credibility of their religion. Believing their faith justified they know that the deafness of unbelievers can never persuade them to jettison it. So much is obvious but the way in which they express themselves among themselves, the actual language which they use, does not have to be the same, so long as it conveys the same message. It is not the words themselves which are sacrosanct but their meaning and the connection between a word and its meaning is never permanently fixed, words associated with one context being frequently commandeered to serve in another. (An example of this is the way that theological terms are now used in order to sell motor cars!) Thus language makes the gap between the opposing worlds wider as a religious minority finds itself confronted by what it regards as the corruption of words and ideas rightly belonging to religion while the rest of society recoils from anything resembling language which implies actual religious belief.

The problem is not simply a linguistic one as the difficulty of communication between religious and secular groups overflows into areas of political discord, particularly in places where there is a high degree of rivalry between social groups identified with particular religions. This may involve them identifying with the religion traditionally associated with the social group or category to which they belong so that whole sections of society, sometimes entire nations, become embroiled in what presents itself as a war of religion. Such things have been happening for centuries, no doubt; nowadays, in places where religion has suffered a loss of credibility, so that nobody is likely to see it as really worth fighting for, such outbreaks of violence are interpreted as proof of the danger of religion itself, as a cause of division likely to result in human misery.

All the same, it is a particularly strong-minded brand of religion that lends itself to this kind of tribalism, one that provides answers more than it permits itself the freedom to ask questions and knows exactly what it believes in and how it believes in it. Even if it could not be seen as actually causing wars, as it could certainly once have been, it still gives the secular world the powerful impression of a rigid and inflexible attitude towards one's fellow human beings. Again, this is not something which accords well with today's post-modern sensibility. For religion to speak effectively to the world nowadays, then it must do so more gently. In particular, it must make fewer demands and with more discretion, showing respect for other kinds of spirituality than its own. It must have more confidence in itself and not be so determined to argue the unarguable. It must depend more on God to fight its battles while it is content to show the love which is acceptance, perhaps not always of ideas but certainly of other people. Our own experience of God is to be shared wherever there is a mutual willingness to listen without the self-defeating urgency which seeks to convince and so often succeeds in alienating. Part of the way we show our love for God is by accepting the necessity to share our joy as he shares his.

Most important of all, we must avoid regarding our own failures as if they were God's. There is an all-too-common assumption that, if there are fewer active members of our faith than there used to be, then this is because God is letting us down. This, again, is part of a failure to love and trust the God in whom we profess to believe; on the one hand, we receive his accepting love; on the other, we refuse to accept the way in which that love chooses to work. What religious organisations so often seem to lack is the confidence that God's work will be done by God. He will carry on doing it in his own way and we must learn to accept that and not keep on striving to make up the shortfall in our own all-too-fallible way. Our failures and defeats are not God's.

Finally, if we want to serve God, we must mirror his love in our acceptance of the necessity to work alongside people we dislike, whether they are fellow members of our own religion with whom we personally disagree or from whom we are estranged for historical reasons, members of other religions than our own, or people of no religion at all who are likely to be the ones we manage to get on with! This may seem easy enough. In fact, it requires tolerance, patience and tact from all involved. All the same it is the service owed to the God of our own acceptance.

CHAPTER 7

So far I have tried to avoid discriminating among the religions I have been writing about. This is because I have tried to confine myself to the theme of religion itself, regarded as the human characteristic of believing in God as a revealed transcendence, the awareness of a presence too detached to be comprehended, yet too intimate to be ignored. The dictionary definition, however, is clear enough: 'Human recognition of superhuman controlling power, and especially of a personal God entitled to obedience' (McIntosh, 1964, 1048). God is personal because he understands and cares for the persons he goes on creating and the world, or worlds, which they inhabit. In other words, he is a God of love, which is the way I have set out to describe him here, for the most part having to confine myself to general statements which may be applied to, or adapted to fit, specific religions. Confining myself to the defining truth of God as Love and abstaining from giving precise details of how this love has manifested itself has not been an easy task but it is one which I felt I must try my persist in..

In doing so I realise that I run the risk of offending the people I am actually writing about. Religious people avoid believing in religion in general, and other religions in particular, by being members of what they hold to be the authentic one, the religion worth believing in compared with which all other faiths, however well-intentioned, do no more than fumble in the dark. This, after all, is what organised religion itself requires from its members in exchange for its assurance of spiritual safety and personal transformation of a kind which has been well documented. No-one could dispute the fact that such benefits are worth having or that the way they are communicated is deeply personal but the exclusiveness of the experience, its unique intimacy, plays upon our need to set ourselves apart from what we may perceive as rival intimacies, particularly those reported by other religions. If this should happen, the law of love may be turned inwards rather than outwards and we find ourselves seeking our own spiritual satisfaction rather than searching out opportunities to exchange joy with other people.

For this is Love's purpose. It asks us to use it not for our purposes but for its own. If we wish to benefit from it, we must give it away, investing it outside the closely guarded territory of self. Loving and caring are synonymous and love itself grows in being shared. If we cling to a cognitive understanding of love, our own definition binds us to itself so that we think perpetually of reasons why we are justified in making exceptions to our theories about love's demands. Surely there must be exceptions to the rule, we say; surely God cannot expect us to love what our religion says we should hate? As all theories have provisos attach to them, the same must be true regarding God and sin; if God hates the sin, then why are we instructed that we should love sinners? If he loves us so much that he has forgiven our sins, he must have a very good reason for excluding them and who are we to question God?

God, however, excludes no-one. Love cannot be love if it excludes. Real belonging is not dependent on threats, even the threat of being excluded. We live in the company of our own sinfulness and that of our fellow human beings within the all-embracing loving acceptance of God. Whether or not we, or other people, sin, God does not change. For those who believe, this is axiomatic. All the same, so far as our actual experience of him goes, it turns out to be a generalisation which calls for much more detail. How, for instance, does this fact apply to us? How does it apply to the world we live in? If we are to take God personally, these are the things we need to know constituting, as they do, essential information regarding the terms of our relationship. We are in no position to require him to enlighten us; so the initiative has to be his own. As we saw in Chapter 6, accounts of action in the world have more meaning for us than abstract information about it. Whether we regard them as historical or figurative, stories capture our imagination to become vehicles of spirit, what the ancient Greeks called *psychopompoi* or messengers conducting our spirits beyond the limitations imposed by this world. Where stories become religious texts they direct our minds and hearts towards the beckoning Spirit of God.

Because of this ability to fuse fact and fiction—the fact of our own experience and the fiction of the story's events and characters—all story-telling is both figurative and historical. When the story concerns God's actions incorporated in the narrative which also involves human beings and other creatures, then an event takes place in which these two opposing story-types coalesce, fiction become history and history fiction. History takes on the reminiscence of events whose meaning and significance exceed those of the things we experience in what we think of as the ordinary world, while being what would otherwise be dismissable as 'only a story' by the living presence in it of the Lord of Truth. The material which makes up religious texts takes the form of a story because this is the way we communicate spiritual messages to best effect. C. S. Lewis (1982, 45), among others, has pointed our the way stories interrupt the flow of time. Certainly, this is so when the story concerns God's relationship with his world which for believers gives it the stamp of faith.

This, then, is the situation regarding religion, that no-one can make sense of it save those for whom it is sense already. For others, it is what they observe it to be—a story. It is a particularly dangerous kind of story because there are those who persist in seeing it as true and who cannot distinguish between fact and fiction. They themselves have stories which they believe to be true and not fictional at all, as the notion of a true story must be a contradiction in terms; their stories, then, are facts. For believers, though, God is a fact and his presence in their story confirms its nature as a story, but one which they can live by. For those who believe in God, his story and their own will now interact, or rather live together in an exchange of love, each confirming the other's reality.

Despite, or rather because of, their nature as stories, their power to convince far outweighs their lack of any kind of worth as scientific or legalistic evidence. The point of a story is not so much what happens as *why* it happens. Why did this happen rather than something else? The point of our religious story-telling is that God has changed human life. Things happening in stories are deliberately arranged to direct attention to the story's message. This is the reason for its being a story to begin with. We want to know why this particular story is being told; what can it be that it is saying to us? As Aristotle claimed, 'the plot is the soul of the tragedy' (Butcher, 1951) and this is true of all stories which set out to capture our imagination and draw us into the action they are describing.

The more important the message, the more vital it is not to allow it to lose itself among everything else which is going on at the time, all the other information we are currently receiving and feel we must deal with, forming a continuous succession of ideas and experiences. We saw in Chapter 2 how the shape of story gives experience itself a memorable quality, helping it to stand out in our minds as something complete in itself. If we have something definite to say, we put it in story form to stop it merging with our landscape of thoughts and feelings. We should not be at all surprised, then, that the liturgies, texts and traditions used by religions to sustain their faith in God should turn to story as their chosen medium of communication. Stories are intellectually refreshing and emotionally fulfilling; within the context of religious faith, they act as sounding-boards for revelation.

All the same, they are still artefacts put together by human beings out of the material at their disposal. Because we ourselves remain human it can hardly be otherwise. As spirit relies upon flesh, so mind reaches for story, each in search of a way to express itself. Stories concerning God's presence among human beings are offered to him as places for him to make himself known to us on his own terms but using our language, the language of our humanity. Thus they possess an identity which is always paradoxical, being constructed, like King Solomon's Temple, as a place for God to dwell even though he who dwells in the heavens has no need of human hands (2 Chr 2). In Solomon's temple an absence proclaims a presence; the former literal, the latter metaphysical as spirit plays host to Spirit. So it is with stories; they too can give flesh to a truth which is ultimate while remaining the product of human imagination. Those who, performing human actions, have known themselves engaged by God are never the same again; their human identity remains unaffected but their awareness of who they are has changed radically. It is this transforming knowledge of God, born of lived experience, which infuses the culture of our religious belonging, whether this is read, spoken or sung. These things are not God himself but our record of our knowledge of him.

We worship God through them, which is not the same as actually worshipping *them*. Their holiness is by association because this is the way our minds work and, when we want to come into the presence of the Extraordinary, we need help to move away from the comfort of ordinariness; here again is the paradox: in order to be with God in the way we have in mind, we seek out things familiar to us which are nevertheless resonant with our experience of him. For example, it is not bread-ness and wine-ness which Christians worship but the crucified and risen Lord who identifies himself with the supper which he is sharing with them.

This paradoxical approach is fundamental to any human knowledge of God. How could it be otherwise? When we allow ourselves to move away from it, we worship things and not God, things we have ourselves made. This is very clear. What is not so obvious, however, is our human responsibility for the things we ourselves deliver. However inspired we may believe ourselves to be, it will always be our version of the message we have received. In the same way, the stories which we compose about ourselves remain our own, although the action of story-making gives them a spiritual significance which can direct us outwards, away from our bondage to the literal. People who feel oppressed by the disjointed nature of their lives are comforted by discovering the ability to see themselves as hero-figures in stories of trial, crisis and deliverance. As a short-term measure this may help to hold things together in times of stress, when our sense of who we know ourselves to be can no longer take the strain, but it remains a story, something not to be confused with any other kind of reality. It may present itself as the actual truth about me, 'the authentic story of my life.' Nevertheless, I made it up myself, and therefore I am in charge of it.

Having created it, I can myself bring it to spiritual life by investing it with my own spirit. This is intended to bring it under my control. Unfortunately, the reverse is liable to happen because, the harder I try to make use of what it is that I have made, the more conscious I am of its power over me. Psychiatrists and psychologists talk of obsessive states of mind and the compulsive nature of neurosis, describing how we are capable of living psychologically in prisons we ourselves have made; but this is more than a trick which the mind plays on itself for we do not simply live in our prisons; we actually *love* them. Where would we be without them? *Who* would we be?

All the same, they do us little good. I may succeed in casting myself as hero of my personal saga; indeed, I may desire some psychological benefit from doing this, particularly in situations in which I would otherwise be overcome by feelings of inadequacy for such is the power of story; but outside the story, I am still myself, still inadequate but now more conscious of the fact as I grow more and more aware of my inability to live up to the myth which I have fashioned for myself. Loving my story is, after all, a way of loving myself. The action is circular so that I am painfully aware of the lack of progress I am making in my search for reassurance. I cannot simply tell myself that I am a worthwhile person—I need to be told.

As the Buddhist poem says, what we ourselves make is the boat. It is no use without the ocean. If we build our boat so that we can launch it, the ocean will be there to take it. Thus, the things we ourselves create, our various forms of story-making, have a purpose beyond ourselves. The boat is a perfect image of this, being built specifically for sailing in. As such it has been used on countless times by poets and story-tellers. The ocean, however, we are not responsible for as only god can make an ocean. This is why seas appeal so powerfully to the artistic imagination as the most telling example of something at one and the same time familiar and unknowable which may be used to symbolise everything beyond our power to tame.

Spiritual imagination (Jung, 1933), which is the creative power of the human spirit, recognises our story-making ability as the gift of God. As with all his gifts, we receive it in order to share it with others, not to turn it in on ourself. In this way, it may be used for love's purposes, as to love the gift is to love the one who is revealed in the giving of it. This is not the satisfaction we have in making things for ourselves but something entirely different, the way our heart lifts at the force of the love we ourselves feel towards another person. This is why stories are so important to those who believe in God, who see their own story-making as his gift, who see their own story as part of the one told by him. Just as in our own stories things fall into place so that they end up making sense to us, so the final, ultimate story tells of the re-ordering of the world in accord with God's purpose of love.

For people who believe in him, their own role in this master story renders it irrelevant whether or not their own story-making is historically accurate. The reality of God's love is mediated through a story of his relationship to the world he has made for himself and others. This may be expressed verbally as a narrative, a metaphor, a statement of belief or pictorially as in an icon or in the form of buildings and locations as with shrines and sacred sites. None of these are meant to contain God and it is their failure to do this that makes them sacred, for the beauty, splendour and mystery they possess speaks to us of a wholeness which cannot be possessed (Grainger, 2004; Post and Molendijk, 2010). They are always the setting for worship, not its actuality, not the drama but its *mise-en-scène*, an absence reminding us of a Presence. However skilfully and devotedly made, however eloquently they speak of God's message, they remain things whereas the God we believe in is alive and within our reach, if not our grasp.

Certainly, no matter how firmly we believe in God, he is never within our grasp. To believe in someone is not to assume that you can somehow control them. Nor does it mean that you have the power to influence them against their own better judgement. What it does involve, however, is a willingness to trust that what they think, say and do will always be in accordance with the trust we have placed in them. In fact, the dictionary defines 'belief' as 'trust,' not a state of intellectual certainty but a movement of the soul, a cry for help from one being to another. The East African villager, anxious for God to send rain, ties a knot in a stalk of maize, not to try and force God's hand but simply to catch his attention, trusting that, whatever God chooses to do, he himself will at least be given a hearing.

Those who believe in God trust not only him but the relationship which they have with him. This is precisely what is meant by believing 'in.' The sacredness of texts, pictures, buildings comes from their identity as pledges of this trust. They are not substitutes for God but reminders of our relationship with him. We have made them for him and their effect on us is a sign of his accepting both gift and giver. All this is mediated by our spiritual awareness of the Image in which we ourselves are made and in which through God's Spirit we live. He certainly does not force us to do this; we are free to live in any image we may choose including our own which, for those who at any time have recognised the presence of God, is idolatry.

Idolatry. This is always a terrifying word, one which makes us look into ourselves to discover whether or not such a thing could possibly apply to us, knowing all the time that it almost certainly could be. The things we do and make belong to us, are made and done by us. We know ourselves to be entirely taken up with them; so for much, or even most, of our lives they are our major concern. Our relationships with other people are affected, even sometimes governed, by them. In the worlds we construct these are the idols we commission to speak for us, sometimes actually to be us. In God's sight, however, they are not us. In fact, they have no effect on God because they are not real, not the truth about us. The effect which they do have is on us.

This, then, is the real danger, that we should come to believe in the things we have made, investing ourselves in our own creativity in order to hide behind it. If we believe in God, we are able to see ourselves doing this. If you asked us why we do it, we would probably say that we didn't want to expose ourselves to charges of inadequacy which we are quite sure would be levelled against us: inadequacy, or something worse, to do with what we ourselves are really like. It is not only religious people who feel like this, of course. We don't really want to be seen that clearly by anybody and, to this extent, it might be said we were natural hiders. Perhaps at some times in our lives we have come out into the open and been rejected. It is more likely, however, that it has been a release, both for ourselves and for those who we feared would turn against us.

Religious people are those who refuse to allow themselves to be defeated by this, although they are conscious of such a mechanism operating in the way in which they set about the business of living. As we have been saying all along, religious people are those who try, at least most of the time, to put God first. They do not always succeed and, in fact, it may be beyond their power to be wholly successful but they are conscious, at the spiritual level, of being led in this direction and of experiencing a particular kind of joy when it happens and their spirit accords with the Spirit of God.

For both idolatry and the determination to turn back from it reflect the conditional nature of human spirit, habitually attuned to choosing whatever seems likely to give the most satisfaction without stopping to ask what real satisfaction would be like. It is not enough simply to let God back into the equation in order to have someone to manipulate or in order to be on the safe side if what people say about him should ever turn out to be true. As to feeling guilty, that could be a sign of grace, so long as we can avoid hugging it to ourselves in an effort to make something of it which we can use to reduce the resentment he surely feels towards us for neglecting him for so long. To sophisticated believers this must appear an extremely childish, even primitive, way of thinking about God. It is certainly primitive but more child-like than child*ish* as it is an honest description of how a religious person may feel under some circumstances and our own spirit assures us that God is only concerned with truth.

Truth is the aim. We know this; yet, almost from the beginning of our lives, both as individuals and as a species, we have found ways of avoiding it, either by straightforward argument or psychological manipulation, convincing ourselves that, for our purposes, a lie would prove more advantageous than the truth; or if not a straightforward lie, then a refusal to consider the evidence. We have eyes and do not see, ears and do not hear (Jr 5:21; see Ps 115:3-6). In other words, we have managed, of our own free will, to make idols of ourselves.

CHAPTER 8

Psychologists describe the urge to concentrate entirely upon one's own needs, thus ignoring the needs of others, as 'narcissism.' Narcissus himself was believed to be the son of a nymph and a river god who was exceptionally proud of his own beauty and particularly of the effect this had on other people. Nemesis, the Goddess of Retribution, determined to punish his vanity by luring him to a pool of water and urging him to gaze upon his reflection in it. Narcissus was entranced by what he saw so that, not realising that the image was of himself, he fell in love with it. Obviously, his love could not be reciprocated as there was no-one else there to do this. All the same he was unable to tear himself away from the beauty of his own reflection so that he eventually died gazing at it.[3]

This is a story about human beings and only secondarily a psychiatric diagnosis. It is about whether our basic concern is with ourselves or something which is not ourself. Our vulnerability forces us into a position where we need help with this and love is our sole support in coming to a decision. If love is there to give us the confidence we must have, we will turn our attention gratefully in its direction and try to give ourselves to trusting it and seeing where it leads us. This is true of all who are capable of exchanging love with others whether of not they see themselves as believing in God. The human spirit is nurtured by the action of donating its own life to others in the interchange of being which depends wholly on trust. This is the law of love which our spirit recognises, however hard we try to dislodge it, by simply giving ourselves to ourselves (Lk 17:33).

We are not only concerned here with those who believe in God but all who have become aware of the dynamics of loving and so managed to steer clear of the spiritual idolatry which involves making oneself in one's own image. It should be pointed out—again—that this is no easy task as the terms on which human beings exist, the limits placed on their physical and emotional capacities, count for so much with regard to the choices which are made by any single individual. Very few of us, I imagine, have been spared times in which our first thoughts have been of ourselves, what we may do to control our panic and deal with the pain, not for a moment reflecting on how the other people involved are feeling, perhaps even refusing their offers of help as we plunge ever more deeply into our own distress.

This, however, comes under the heading of ontological vulnerability rather than narcissism (Tillich, 1962). What we have been considering is no immediate reaction to intolerable emotional or physical agony but an established frame of mind, the well-entrenched habit of gazing on our own image and seeing no reason to look in any other direction than our own. This, surely, is idolatry of the human spirit but even here the same applies as with implicit religion, that it can only be given the significance it undoubtedly possesses in the bible when it represents the frame of mind, or condition of soul, of someone who professes to believe in God. Here self is being substituted for an absence that has not been allowed to exist; when such an absence is acknowledged, the human spirit reaches out for whatever is culturally available and has social prestige or personal significance.

Idolatry depends on taking God seriously but not actually trusting him, so that we are willing to try something which may turn out to be more biddable, particularly so as we have made it ourselves; and apart from this the state of affairs when we believe ourselves to be in the hands of the real God has become intolerable so that we may be disposed to look elsewhere for support. Even then we have a choice, however, because our spirit tells us that there is a purpose in our suffering, one which is in line with God's Spirit, and we should go on trusting whatever happens. God is aware of our pain and will bring us relief, as he has done so often in the past when, in our despair, we turned to him for help. All the same, there is a limit to what even the most committed believers can put up with and never falter. We are, after all, human and cannot tolerate too much pain, however much we may pretend.

So we may worship God, or something we ourselves have made. There is a third option, however, in which we try to do both at the same time. It was this which angered Jeremiah so much:

> Will you . . . make offerings to Baal, and go after other gods you have not known, and then come and stand before me in this house, which is called by my name, and say, 'We are safe!'—only to go on doing all these abominations? (Jr 7:8-10).

'We are safe!' The logic is inescapable; if having one god means security for the believer, then how much better will he or she be protected from harm by having several? Jeremiah's 'abominations' were all regarded as gods, having had divinity thrust upon them by their worshippers in accordance with the human capacity for god-making; it was not wood and stone which was being adored but the god whom they represented. If the prophet had perceived his fellow citizens worshipping wood as wood, or stone as stone, he would have accused them of stupidity, not blasphemy. The offence lay in their assumption that gods might be controlled, or at least influenced, by being addressed though images. If Yahweh could not—and that was what the temple was all about, certainly—then perhaps other gods could? It was at least worth trying.

Put like this, the situation may sound amusing. Jeremiah, however, was not amused and neither should we be. The temptation to 'hedge our bets' presents itself in various ways even though we are sure of the God we believe in. We may not recognise its working because the impulse to protect ourselves against the danger of things going wrong is intrinsic to our nature as human beings. Left to ourselves we automatically choose the safest option. We set out to succeed and tell ourselves that is always means hard work but why we actually do work so hard is because the idea of failure is intolerable to us and must at all costs be avoided. Those who say that they trust God and proceed to take no other precautions may expect to receive a good deal of criticism, and not all of it from unbelievers. Most people, it seems, whether religious or not, refuse to see any connection between not relying on God and making sure their insurance policy is up-to-date.

The fact remains, however, that to trust God and something else as well might be seen, on a strict reckoning, as a form of idolatry, 'implicit idolatry' perhaps. Unlike those who practice implicit religion, implicit idolaters confess to being religious. What they sometimes find hard to admit, however, is that they may not always be whole-heartedly so. However they may explain their situation themselves, their loyalties are divided. It may be, of course, that they are unaware of the fact so that the discovery that they have been putting something else before God will come as a shock to them and they will be moved to try and do what they can to put things right. They will have to do this on their own as society itself is unlikely to give them any help. Setting God above activities aimed at increasing human prestige is, for us, decidedly counter-cultural!

In any case, it would be invidious to try and compare life in a society whose values are almost entirely secular with the state of affairs in one organised in line with strict religious observance. The idolatry of Jeremiah's contemporaries stands out clearly within the setting of the Jerusalem Temple whereas the tendency of religious people to be alarmed at the strength of their loving involvement with creatures appears far-fetched when we consider God's own evident delight in all that he has made. If our embarrassment on this score causes us to concentrate all the more closely on God, so much the better, but our knowledge of him would lead us to believe that the love we show others is itself a crucially important way of serving him. In circumstances in which an explicitly religious approach can only alienate, the language of love creates its own response.

For one thing, the connection beloved of sociologists between religious belonging and social acceptability is less clear now than it has ever been before, or at least that is what is generally supposed to be the case, although religious behaviour itself has shifted focus and now attaches itself to social phenomena of a non-religious kind. It is, however, still behaviour motivated by love and, even though it is not explicitly directed towards God himself, it is towards aspects of his activity, people and things which exist because of him and are loved and cherished by him. Such relationships with the created world are not forced on us; they are the result of a determination to trust what cannot be controlled and to respond to the call made on their feelings by whatever it is that reaches out to them. Religious people may see this as idolatry and I have been arguing that the charge is undeserved because there is no intention to create a rival to God in which one does not in any case believe. I myself was quite firm on the point.

But is it true? If belief in God is a habit of mind which turns out in certain circumstances to be unsustainable in the face of what appears to be convincing evidence, then finding a substitute and trusting oneself to it, whatever it may be, would hardly count as idolatry, considering the human spirit's participation in the creativity of God. This, however, is not the only way of believing as, for some people, to transfer their loyalties in such a way is not an option they would ever consider. These are those whose belief is, in the very deepest sense of the word, personal. Whatever happens to them in life, their loyalty remains firm: God *is*, and they belong to him. Mere argument to the contrary will never shake them. The idolatry we have been considering is beside the point. What they love in the world, they love for God's sake so that their faith embraces everyone, those who think of themselves as religious and those who do not.

Up to now I have used the word 'religious' to stand for any person who believes in God. This is because my aim has been to address the difference between two kinds of worshipper, those who put their trust in God and those who invest themselves elsewhere. I have tried to concentrate on the subject of believing in God in a way which is applicable to more than one religion but I doubt that I have really managed to do this very well because of my own definite commitment to an understanding of God which is specifically Christian. What I have been saying concerns religious systems which revolve round God as Creator Spirit, as these find the notion of gods put together by human beings particularly distasteful, particularly to those whose faith is genuinely personal and yet takes within its scope the whole of creation. But even this kind of religion is open to one brand of idolatry and that a particularly subversive one which is able to strike right to the heart of faith because it appears to be so entirely reasonable. It is the fetish we make of competence, of being equipped to deal with any eventuality which could possibly arise.

This is not faith. Nor is faith simply the power to survive difficulties of a spiritual nature. Faith is what we cling to despite our inability to cope when things go desperately wrong. It is what we have when we are aware of having little else. Because it is spiritual, it resists attempts at regularisation, so that we can never be sure of the way it operates as we would like to be able to be. Anything we may think up to make sure of it is an idol we ourselves have made; if we put our trust in it we inevitably do so at faith's expense. Faith cannot be forced so that we are bound to seek safety in things that can, having been made precisely for that purpose. It is only when these fail that faith comes into its own. Faith is the essence of religion because it requires us to trust God and not ourselves, however terrifying this may be for us. In contrast to this, a society which has abandoned God worships its own ability to succeed without him and the way to do this is to make certain nothing can ever go wrong without immediately being put right, preferably before anyone has actually noticed. In such a world-view, not knowing what to do to fix something is always to some extent an admission of failure and therefore something of which a person ought to be ashamed.

This is nothing new, of course. In order to be able to survive on earth, human beings have always had to be 'fixers.' As their ability to manipulate their environments increased, so did their sense of self-sufficiency and the need to turn to God for help in the practical business of living became less urgent, and divine assistance was only sought for matters concerning the spiritual life of individuals and communities. God became a last resort when all other solutions had proved inadequate. His serviceability had been eroded by mankind's capability. There was no longer 'any need for that hypothesis.'[4] However, from the late nineteenth century onwards there was a general tendency to find God useless, not only among scientists, but with regard to the rapidly growing number of those amazed and delighted by the discoveries which were being made concerning the ways in which the real world of things and people could be shown to function and the potentially limitless possibilities this offered for bringing it under control.

Although science does not claim to be a religion, and many scientists would be appalled by the suggestion that it should ever seek to be one, nevertheless it certainly has some of the characteristics of religious belief, particularly in the behaviour of those devoted to its characteristic view of life which conforms very closely to the paradigm set forward by Edward Bailey and others.[5] The way in which scientific values are able to shape the behaviour and attitudes of individuals and societies allows science to take on the role of the key to life, the organising principle which holds our world together. Just as everything concerning humanity is theoretically open to scientific scrutiny, so science itself is able to focus human efforts to achieve the mastery of which we are inherently capable and which is our destiny.

These things are assumed rather than argued. For most educated western European people, they are too obvious to need defending. In any case, why apologise for a view of humanity which reveals us as God's successors? It may well be, as some have said, that the decline of explicit religions belief has opened the way for a greater sensitivity to the worth of human beings as themselves rather than as characters in a divine drama. The fact that, in a rationalistic age, we still behave as if we were religious, seeking for places and situations, organisations and personalities in which to invest our spirit, is surely evidence that the religious impulse is able to survive society's determination to treat it as redundant, if not actively dangerous, and even now there are those who cling to ideas and practices that are totally and unashamedly religious in the most explicit way. Unlike Jeremiah's Temple worshippers, they refuse to believe in God while keeping on the safe side by availing themselves of man-made means of protection. On the contrary, they are determined to put their trust only in God. As Jeremiah said of these faithful followers of Yahweh who stayed on in Jerusalem after most of the nation had been taken into exile in Babylon, they are 'the saving remnant' (Jr 23:3).

I am not talking only about those whose religion is the same as mine. The sense of isolation, of living in a spiritually alien world, extends far beyond the walls of church, mosque, temple or synagogue. It is a burden borne by religious people everywhere. An incident stands out in my memory of the time in my own life when I worked as a hospital chaplain, when a young Muslim doctor stopped me in the corridor after we had been holding a service on one of the wards. 'I'm glad that someone in this place believes in God,' he said. (He wasn't accusing anyone of being atheists, just scientists.)

Nowadays people of faith are aware of belonging together to a degree which they never did before. At least, this is the situation in large parts of the world, especially in secular societies such as western Europe and North America. This is because the situation in which they find themselves has started to change as it becomes obvious that the differences among religions can no longer be considered as important as that between religious people and those who claim to have no religion at all. What is not so obvious is that absence of belief in God does not in fact leave society without religion; it simply means that they start to have one of their own, one which they themselves have created.

CHAPTER 9

Let him who glories glory in this, that he
understands and knows *me* (Jr 9:24)

This, again, is Jeremiah; a New Testament version of it occurs
when Jesus heals the paralysed man:

How can you believe when you receive glory from
one another and do not seek the glory that comes
from the only God? (Jn 5:44).

Jesus is defending his action against those accusing him of
breaking a religious law by working on the Sabbath. He states very
plainly that laws formulated for God's service are not intended
to add to the satisfaction of those professing to keep them but
to carry out the purposes of love. In the life of faith some things
are more important than others. It is these 'other things'—
history, tradition, social acclaim, the effects of persecution or
state patronage—which get in the way of love. Love is the law
which abides when all other laws are broken. Its reward is love,
not social prestige.

What gets in the way most turns out to be our abuse of free
will, striking at the place of our greatest vulnerability, our power

to invent our own kinds of religion. It doesn't matter what we call them; they reflect our own importance. When we give ourselves in worship to what we ourselves have made, or believe we can make in the future, we exchange the image of God for one of ourselves. Those who are unwilling to contrive a more convenient religion than the one which they inherited are brought into a new kind of relationship with one another, of a kind unknown to former generations, the alliance of those who worship God and not just his creatures, believing that those made in the image of God should not be so eager to disown him, having invented what they believe to be a more effective, and certainly more reassuring, substitute. Those who have received in their own spirit the message from Spirit that only God can help them and the assurance that it is his joy to do so will not easily turn to support which is man-made, no matter how much they care for their fellow human beings. Because they themselves know that it is their answering love for God which causes them to love his creatures, they are particularly aware of the disillusion awaiting those who put their trust in anything else apart from God, seeking his help in sharing what they themselves so freely receive.

This, after all, is their greatest joy—or, at least, it should be. We have seen how counter-productive their efforts appear to have been so far as contemporary life goes. All the same, as we have seen, the effect of secularisation need not be to destroy faith—it is unable to do that—but to re-direct it. As Bailey suggests, the failure of doctrinal religions to capture our imagination to the extent of previous generations may be due to the appeal of a kind of secular humanism which is religious in fact but not in name, expressing itself in an increased sensitivity to the needs of others, a case of doing religion without believing in it, or not in its traditional, easily recognisable form (Bailey, 2001). To an outside observer this might appear as something to be welcomed by organised religions who never cease to proclaim God's love for mankind and should welcome support from all who show a loving respect towards it from any direction whatever.

Unfortunately the situation is not so simple. One reason for this is the determination on the part of those who belong to a religion to proclaim their loyalty to a living personal God. To abstain from doing this would appear to be, at best, a betrayal or, at worst, an act of blasphemy. This being so, they are likely to reject any suggestion that they should consider forming an alliance with those who regard God as an outworn idea, one which no longer has any relevance. Centuries of conflict within religion itself as to which story about God's relationship with his world was to be believed would obviously add to the difficulty of clarifying what it was exactly that people were proposing to agree about. The second difficulty, therefore, would be vagueness and lack of personal impact. The third, however, would be extremely personal, because it would involve one of our basic human needs, that of belonging to a group of people with whom we identify.

Religions welcome converts. Indeed they profess to a willingness to enrol anybody so long as they promise to obey the rules which specify the terms of belonging. They see this as acting in conformity with God's revealed will. However, it is also a way in which human beings naturally behave as individual identity and group membership are interdependent: I know who I myself am because I can distinguish people with whom I think I have something in common from others who are in some way or another different from me. Those like me already form a group with me and I with them, even before we have actually made personal contact, so that the experience of identifying myself as a group member is a reassuring one, offering itself to me as a kind of home-coming. The feeling of solidarity which comes from belonging with one's fellow spirits is something which we all enjoy. Although we would like others to be able to participate, we also want to keep it for ourselves.

In terms of stress, the second impulse strives for dominance so that it assumes control of the situation. An example of this happening within a religious setting would be the reaction of the Roman Catholic Church to the liberalising reforms instituted by the Second Vatican Council (1962-65), which resulted in several decades of extreme conservatism on the part of the Catholic magisterium. With the Christian church as a whole change is regarded as potentially dangerous and revision of social rules is considered to be more threatening than anything else because it seems to undercut the Church's authority as the sole arbiter of social values. This will not be so with every religion, of course, but the principle remains binding on all actual members of religious groups—that faith is to be lived out in social practices which identify someone as somebody who belongs to a particular religion and wishes to proclaim this fact about themselves.

But to be recognisable is also be vulnerable. The more secularised society becomes, the more religious people seek to identify themselves as members of their religion which they see as somehow under siege. Their faith is more precious to them and also more dangerous. What it has to offer is uniquely valuable and must at all costs be preserved and yet they are conscious of the soul's need to reach beyond itself and take courage from what it knows to be God's purposes for mankind. This is something which concerns not only one particular religion but all of them. It is impossible to be defensive and adventurous at the same time but this is the position in which in some parts of the world we currently find ourselves.

It is also, of course, how God finds us. Just as he searches for individuals who feel that they have gone off course, so he works with communities which have managed to lose their way. He is, after all, used to chaos. With him, though, it is necessary for us to take chances as defensiveness cripples action. God does not force us to move but he does encourage us to trust in his purpose for us. This certainly does not mean changing the terms of our own commitment, abandoning our story for one less explicitly religious. What it does mean, however, is that we should learn how to be religious in a different way. In those places where, for cultural reasons, worshipping God is no longer regarded as making sense so that the spiritual life of women and men is invested in one another—for spirit must always find somewhere to rest—the love which ensues holds us all in its arms and does not make distinctions. So long as we possess the spiritual capacity to love, the love we have prevails. Where there is intellectual disagreement or the memory of past wrongs, the Spirit of God is present in acts of reconciliation; where there is fear or apathy, he brings hope.

So, in the words of an American President, 'the only thing we have to fear is fear itself' (Franklin D Roosevelt, First Inauguration Address 4 March 1933). Religion itself, our own or anyone else's, is in not danger. The things we fear are human ones: anxiety concerning our own personal relationship with God and our failure to safeguard our heritage for others. Above all, we fear our own inability to cope with our feelings of depression and our sense of disillusion. God knows these things and helps us with them whether or not we are in a position to recognise the fact. We think it is because we see ourselves as defenders of religion that we must bear these burdens but our pain is the same as anyone else's when it comes to parting with the things we love.

All the same, it is not our religion that we are in the process of leaving behind but only some of the things associated with it which we ourselves have persisted in bringing to it. We are used to thinking of these in terms of traditional forms of worship, sacred texts, devotional practices, items of apparel, but in fact none of these need necessarily be jettisoned so long as they are not allowed to get in the way of more important matters or, rather, if they may become the symbols of a more generous and whole-hearted awareness. What religious people have brought to religion is a determination to organise it. It is as if they thought that whatever happened it must be protected from itself. Because it concerns God it needs the weight of human organisations, human definitions, to hold it down and keep it securely in place.

But where is its place? The answer is everywhere, of course. Religion's tendency is identical to that of the world. If the words we use and the structures we erect point beyond themselves, praising God by means of their own inadequacy, they perform their function rightly. If they define the nature of God in case it should be misunderstood, they put themselves at the mercy of those who, for epistemological reasons, ones to do with what is allowed to count as evidence, are not equipped to understand in any case. Religion must learn not to hamper itself when associating with those who are not religious by persisting in claiming the right to use a language that is unintelligible to people outside the charmed circle of religious instruction, not only unintelligible but in the contemporary intellectual climate frequently dismissed as nonsensical—even dangerously so. Religious belief fits neatly into the category of 'meta-narratives,' interpretations of, or stories about, the life of human beings which have assumed a position of dominance in society to the exclusion of any other ways of thinking—explanations of everything in which nothing is permitted to make sense except in, and on, their terms. In this religion is not the only offender, simply the most obvious one; scientific, political and economic theories may perform the same function or even doctrines concerning education or childbirth. The force of such ideas lies in their simplicity; they present themselves as both simple and incontrovertible, almost self-evident, an end to having to search for ways of making sense of things, perhaps a relief from having having to think for oneself at all; where the truth leads, we must follow.

Nowadays we are particularly conscious of the danger of this attitude, so that people tend to be wary of becoming imaginatively involved in any one point of view to the extent of giving it their own personal allegiance. Ideas should always be our servants and never our masters. By promoting one commanding position of being able to ride roughshod over any signs of opposition, any thoughts, feelings or attitudes of mind which run contrary to it, we disqualify ourselves from using one of the most precious of our human abilities, the capacity to think round things and arrive at compromise solutions in cases where lack of flexibility would result in disaster. If whatever it is that has usurped our power to withstand the force of its logic should come up against something as rigidly organised as itself, the result will always be a serious loss of freedom, sometimes resulting in wars, which neither side thought they would have to fight, or oppressive regimes set up for what appeared to be the best of reasons.

Totalitarian thought may be demonstrated as leading to totalitarian action; but can human beings ever be that sure of themselves? Increasing knowledge of how the mind works and what actually constitute the springs of human action make it more difficult ever to be dictatorial about how rational our conclusions are, how unaffected by contextual factors and prior suppositions

(Lyotard, 1984). What may be put forward as indisputable may, from another perspective, appear highly doubtful. We are in no position to legislate about other people's truth. No wonder, then, that we are told so often that firm opinions are fraudulent since there can be no valid reason why any one person's view of reality should be set above anyone else's, except of course that of the person engaged in putting the argument across. It is not one which religious people will take seriously unless it is made quite clear that God is not meant to be included within its terms of reference. Even then, it seems to be imposing a burden on people to say that they must avoid regarding anything as true in itself in case its truth somehow carries them away and they start trying to impose it on others. The human mind is geared to making sense of things and the wider a truth is the more attractive it appears because it may be used to answer so many questions.

Too many, in fact, so that we end up with one dominating world-view, a 'regnant construct' (Kelly, 1991) from whose position everything is argued and to which everything returns. Mind and spirit work together to create a situation in which life is perpetually seen through the same pair of spectacles and other ways of understanding are occluded and consequently ignored. Our yearning for spiritual fulfilment, our innate capacity for worship are locked in a single direction. Whether or not we see ourselves as religious is beside the point. If we are members of a religion, it is to be hoped that our God is one of love and that he or she is more loving than we are so that we may catch it from him.

This is the way in which rationalist society regards religious people, It is why it imagines them to be dangerous for it has been convincingly shown over many centuries that they can only see things from one point of view: their own. In fact, of course, there are as many religious points of view as there are religions.

Whether those of us whose lives have been transformed by our commitment to one of them agree with this judgement is not the issue. We may have to admit that some of the charges brought against religion in general—and our own in particular—are well founded. If we are unwilling to do this, we will quite reasonably be seen as providing even more evidence against ourselves. In any case, arguing about religion is almost as counter-productive as arguments among religions. Faith is not about argument. This is something religious people know, even though they frequently appear to forget the fact. Religion is about love. The fruit of God's Spirit, say Paul, is 'love, joy, peace, patience, kindness, generosity, faithfulness, gentleness and self-control' (Ga 15:22-23). St Paul is writing as a Christian but what he says is true of all who put their trust in God.

For such people, religion is the action of opening the heart to God. Every year representatives of Baha'i, Brahma Kumaris, Buddhism, Christianity, Hinduism, Islam, Jainism, Judaism and Zoroastrianism meet in London to celebrate what they all share as children of a loving God.[6] Each faith speaks for itself in terms of its own religious tradition. Together they proclaim the fact that, although religion has contributed to wars, its purpose is for the peace and love which is our obedience to God. This is only one example of a movement throughout the world which is aimed at bringing home to people what religion is actually about—not a particular religion but all of them, the relationship with God which gives meaning and hope to our relationships with one another. Although at first sight this movement may give the impression that it is mainly concerned with improving relations among religions, its main purpose is to speak up on behalf of religion itself.

During the last twenty years western philosophy has shifted its impetus back from a positivist determination to identify a single ruling principle within human thought towards Kant's position which was to assert the subjective nature of knowledge and understanding (Kant, 2010). It is claimed that since the 'Age of Enlightenment' in the eighteenth century the western world has been dominated by a succession of 'final solutions,' each of them representing the latest, most innovative approach to life: 'the way we do things now we really understand how everything works.' Examples of this spring readily to mind: Marxist-Leninism and fascism, for instance, in the political world, psychoanalysis and behaviourism in psychology, genetic determinism in biological science. Each of these, and many more, have been presented as the modern, enlightened way of proceeding. Each of them has paid the penalty attached to appearing to promise too much, sometimes with results which have proved fatal, particularly when they contradict one another, each claiming to be the only intelligible source of understanding.

'Modernism' then concentrates entirely on one line of thought, that in which the original breakthrough into enlightenment took place. 'Post-modernism'—which now dominates philosophical thought in a very modern way—is a reaction against this and, instead of setting out to cut the Gordian knot[7] of the world with one single stroke, is determined to see other attitudes towards the task of making sense of life as philosophically valid. Universal reason, existing by itself independently of the minds operating according to its principles, must now share its authority with emotional understanding and human intuition. Post-modern writers and thinkers talk of the 're-enchantment of the world' after the disillusionment which followed the collapse of faith in a culture which never ceased to promise total success and yet repeatedly failed to do so.

During the last decades, the stranglehold of a reductive rationalism in all aspects of society in the western world has been loosened, at least in academic circles. Science can now be seen as a part of life rather than as all of it, so that matters lying beyond its grasp may now be taken seriously without being held up to ridicule or regarded with suspicion as potential threats to the authority of scientific orthodoxy. In many areas of life spiritual experience is now respectable where it would previously have run the risk of a psychiatric diagnosis. Nowadays even people who do not consider themselves to be religious acknowledge it as part of the truth about being human. At first sight, post-modernism appears to be aimed against religion itself as a 'meta-narrative' which constrains and limits thought—and indeed that is how most religious people react to it—but in fact it only concerns the kind of religious attitude of mind that is defensively organised, repudiating the claims of other world-views to have any share in the spiritual truth which motivates human beings and refusing to discuss the matter.

Of the two positions, embattled defensiveness and the God-confidence which attempts to treat those with whom one disagrees with empathy, the second embodies rejection of the rigorous imposition of obedience to the rule of an idea which has caused so much human suffering in past ages. Whatever that rule was, it was not the law of love. As religions people we can afford to be generous for we have nothing to fear from the acceptance of diversity. In fact, we can learn from it to love those whom we are used to treating as our enemies—not only ours but God's. In this way we may give room to Holy Spirit and follow where God is actually leading us.

Such has been the aim of the present book. Religion has only one priority, which is to concern people with God. The book rests on a single proposition: that God and love are one and the same. Creating, sustaining, reconciling, forgiving, restoring, renewing, returning, transforming are all love; so is caring and all the suffering attached to it. The spirit's yearning and God's Spirit rejoicing are love; so are nurturing and having patience. All these things, and other more elusive things not so easily tied down, are love for, in fact, love itself is not being constrained; so freedom is love too. I write as a Christian; so my experience of God is embedded in the presence of Jesus Christ and I myself am aware of living in his story. This quintessential personal experience of being 'seized by the story' characterises the human reality of religion as God who is Spirit draws close to our own spirits in order to pass on a story regarding himself. This is no vague idea or abstract truth like 'trust' or even 'love' but something which we can latch onto. The stories are not identical because they are personal; they are stories for *us*. They will not agree in detail or according to the response which we are called to make to them but they are the story we share with God as our imagination cooperates with his Spirit. In them he incorporates his creative love towards us.

When someone is telling a story we who owe so much to story-telling should sit down with them and listen. So far as other religions than our own are concerned, the things we agree upon are many and precious and deserve our close attention always. These things we celebrate by simply listening. But we should also listen when we hear the secular world telling its own story which always, either explicitly or implicitly, involves us too. Perhaps that is why it is so very important for us to listen properly because the level of understanding which exists between us is so painfully low and each side needs to pay more attention to what the other has to say. In such a case as this, disagreement turns out to be even more precious than agreement for, to listen properly is itself a loving action, and love is highly contagious.

During this book I have often drawn attention to the vital role played by stories in our lives. At the same time I have been anxious about doing this in case it should be thought I was referring to fiction rather than fact for this seems to be an assumption which is commonly made when we talk about stories and story-telling. There is no reason why religious people should do so for the story we tell is not something to which we ourselves have given life. On the contrary it is we who are made fully alive by taking part in it. When we commit ourselves to a story we make it our own to the extent that we identify ourselves with that we find there. We can stand back from it in order to inspect it just as we can with the story we are engaged in living but what we are looking at in this detached way is more than just an object; it is a potential subject. Sometimes, led by God's own Spirit, it takes up residence with us in that central story-place to which we have been summoned, which is temple, workshop and playroom. Our faith is not a story we tell about ourselves but the story told about ourselves in which we ourselves live. As such it is the place where we form relationships and make friends—not *a* story, *the* story.

And so we come back to the human spirit without which there would be no religious awareness at all, not even the conscious absence of religion. In such a case we would not be the people whom God has made in his own image; we could not respond to him and be in a human relationship with him. There is nothing automatic about this. We are not in any way forced into it. How could it be a personal relationship if that were the case? The American psychotherapist, G. G. May (1982, 32) describes the human spirit as 'that aspect of our fundamental essence which gives it power.' Our spirit works as a search engine for the soul's image of God for, as St Augustine addresses God in the *Confessions* (Bk 1), 'our heart is restless until it finds its rest in you.' This is true of all religions, not only the ones that we ourselves have been called to and to which we have given our heart, mind and imagination. As Lois Lang-Sims puts it:

> It is our own tradition, whether this be Christian, Islam, Jewish, Hindu or Buddhist or any other, that has been validated down the ages by the witness of its sages and saints that has formed their structured patterns in our minds that respond to its symbolism, as one dances in a certain way to certain kinds of music (1988).

Religion itself is a crystallisation of the encounter between spirit and Spirit. More than anything else it is a fulfilment, *the* fulfilment. Because it enshrines God's Spirit, it cannot be changed by anything else. Only we, our individual, personal spirits, can be changed by its action through our searching and the way we respond to what the search has revealed—the way we can now think about it and tell its story. 'A spiritual guest,' says May,'becomes decidedly religious only when one begins to identify a relation with the Ultimate Spirit,' and he adds, 'when that relationship begins to manifest itself in specific behaviors and as worship' (1982, 33), as it has done in the past and continues to do even now.

With this in mind we should, finally, consider another kind of idolatry, one which attracts less attention than those mentioned above but which is nonetheless both insidious and pervasive. Its relevance is immediately obvious, although we try hard to ignore its presence in ourselves. This is the idolatry of knowing better. Certainly this has been going on within and among us for a considerable time, ever since Eden, in fact. It pervades western culture in the form of our worship of the intellect, expressed in the way we structure our educational systems and formulate rules for the division of labour. For religious people, it means depending on statistics rather than on God. 'Lord, this is impossible,' we say. 'Just look at the evidence.' So he does, but not from the same angle. He sees our confusion and distress and knows the way we think and its limitations. From the other side of thought, he heals our troubled souls.

> I give you a new commandment, that you love one
> another. Just as I have loved you (Jn 13:34).

Those who hear the message which God gives to his world approach that world carrying the richness of their story with them, not to dispute but to share. This is a fundamental truth about religion itself which we frequently find reasons for overlooking. The time has come for a radical shift of focus. We can no longer assume that, because in one way or another most people may be thought of as believing in God, the most important thing is to believe in him in the right way, which means the way which we personally have made our own. We can no longer go on pretending, as we have for so long, that the heart of religion itself concerns the difference in the way various religions analyse their experience of God's love. Loyalty to the unique status of one's own revelation can easily cause us to overlook the reason why the revelation was given in the first place: not to cause division but to bring peace. The gulf which exists between religious traditions is still less important than the opportunity for love which it creates for us as we learn to look at one another as fellow servants of God.

'Thank goodness there's someone here who believes in God.' The doctor's words show his skill as a diagnostician. The wound to be tackled first of all is not that between Muslims and members of other religions, but that between those who believe in God and those who don't. In Love, and the wound which it makes, is our healing.

NOTES

Chapter 4

[1] Daniel Johnson (2012) writes that it 'cannot be found in any of his works and appears to have begun life as a paraphrase by his biographer Emile Cammaerts.'

[2] 'idol. n. Image of deity used as object of worship' (McIntosh, 1964, 602).

Chapter 8

[3] The classic version of the story is by Ovid in his *Metamorphoses*, Book 3 (2004).

[4] The quotation 'I have no need of that hypothesis' is from the French mathematician, Pierre-Simon Lagrange's criticism of Isaac Newton's belief that God was needed to correct 'errors' in planetary motion.

[5] The formal study of Implicit Religion began in 1968. It concentrates on those aspects of everyday life the understanding of which may be enhanced by asking whether they might have some sort of inherent religiosity of their own—a kind of 'secular faith.' The journal *Implicit religion* is published four times a year by Equinox Publishing Ltd, Unit S3 Kelham House, 3 Lancaster Street, Sheffield, S3 8AF, U.K.

Chapter 9

6   http://weekofprayerforworldpeace.com/

7   It was said of the Gordian knot that whoever could untie it would rule all Asia. Alexander the Great used his sword to slice through it.

BIBLIOGRAPHY

'Abdu'l-Bahá (1990). *The secret of divine civilization*. Wilmette, IL: US Bahá'í Publishing Trust.

Augustine, Saint, Bishop of Hippo (1972). *Confessions*. Menston: Scolar Press. Translated from the Latin by Sir Tobias Matthew.

Bailey, E. I. (1997). *Implicit religion in contemporary society*. Kampen NL: Kok Pharos.

Bailey, E. I. (2001). *The secular faith controversy: religion in three dimensions*. London: Continuum.

Baxter, E. (2013, Autumn). Reflections on embodied approaches to spiritual direction. *Chrism 5*(2). Proceedings of Holy Rood House Centre for the Study of Theology.

Bettis, J. D. (Ed.) (1969). *Phenomenology of religion: eight modern descriptions of the essence of religion*. London: SCM Press.

Bishop, P. (2013). Seeing with the eyes of the Spirit. *Guild Papers: the Guild of Pastoral Psychology* (313).

Bowlby, E. J. M. (1971). *Attachment and loss: Vol. 1 Attachment*. Harmondsworth: Penguin.

Buber, M. (1958). *I and thou*. Edinburgh: T & T Clark. Translated by Ronald Gregor Smith.

Butcher, S. H. (1951). *Aristotle's theory of poetry and fine art: with a critical text and a translation of the Poetics* (Fourth ed.). New York: Dover.

Carroll, L. (1876). *The hunting of the snark: an agony in eight fits.* London: Macmillan.

Church of England. Liturgical Commission (1999). *Common worship: collects and post communions in traditional language.* London: Church House.

Congreve, W. (1697). *The mourning bride* (Second ed.). London: Jacob Tonson.

Dawkins, R. (2007). *The God delusion.* London: Black Swan.

Dickinson, E. (1970). *The complete poems: edited by Thomas H. Johnson.* London: Faber and Faber.

Durkheim, É. (1915). *The elementary forms of the religious life: a study in religious sociology* . . . London: George Allen & Unwin.

Eliade, M. (1958). *Patterns in comparative religion.* London: Sheed and Ward. Translation by Rosemary Sheed of (1949) *Traité d'histoire des religions,* Paris: Payot.

Emerson, R. W. (1910). *Essays and English traits.* Harvard Classics, Vol. 5 Edited by Charles W. Eliot. New York: P F Collier & Sons.

Frankl, V. E. (1977). *The unconscious God: psychotherapy and theology.* London: Hodder and Stoughton.

Frisby, D. and M. Featherstone (Eds.) (1997). *Simmel on culture: selected writings.* London: SAGE.

Gendlin, E. T. (1981). *Focusing: how to gain direct access to your body's knowledge* (Second ed.). London: Bantam. Quoted in Baxter (2013).

Grainger, R. (1974). *The language of the rite.* London: Darton, Longman and Todd.

Grainger, R. (2004). *Response and responsibility: the world as a challenge for the Church.* Peterborough: Epworth Press.

Grof, S. (1985). *Beyond the brain: birth, death, and transcendence in psychotherapy.* Albany NY: State University of New York Press.

Haddon, M. (2013). *The red house.* London: Vintage.

Harter, M. (Ed.) (2005). *Hearts on fire: praying with Jesuits.* Chicago: Loyola Press.

Hastings, J., J. A. Selbie, and L. H. Gray (Eds.) (1926). *Encyclopaedia of religion and ethics: Vol.10, Picts—Sacraments.* Edinburgh: T & T Clark.

Heidegger, M. (1996). *Being and time.* Albany NY: State University of New York Press. Translation by Joan Stambaugh of *Sein und Zeit.*

Hopkins, G. M. (1996). *Poems and prose.* London: D Campbell.

James, W. (1929). *The varieties of religious experience: a study in human nature: being the Gifford Lectures on Natural Religion delivered at Edinburgh, etc.* London: Longmans & Co.

Johnson, D. (2012, March). Overrated: Umberto Eco. *Standpoint* (40), 78.

Joyce, J. (1960). *A portrait of the artist as a young man.* Harmondsworth: Penguin.

Jung, C. G. (1933). *Modern man in search of a soul.* London: Kegan Paul & Co. Translated by W. S. Dell and Cary F. Baynes.

Jung, C. G. (1938). *Psychology and religion.* New Haven CT: Yale University Press.

Kant, I. (2010). *Critique of pure reason.* Hazleton, PA: Pennsylvania State University. Translation by J. M. D. Meiklejohn of (1786) *Critik der reinen Vernunft* Jena.

Kelly, G. A. (1991). *The psychology of personal constructs: Vol. 1. A theory of personality Vol. 2. Clinical diagnosis and psychotherapy.* London: Routledge.

Lang-Sims, L. (1988). *One thing only: a Christian guide to the universal quest for God.* Paragon House.

Lévi-Strauss, C. (1970). *The raw and the cooked: introduction to a science of mythology.* London: Jonathan Cape. Translation of *Le cru et le cuit.*

Lewis, C. S. (1982). *Of this and other worlds: edited by Walter Hooper.* London: Collins.

Lyotard, J.-F. (1984). *The postmodern condition: a report on knowledge.* Manchester: Manchester University Press. Translation of *La Condition postmoderne* by Geoff Bennington and Brian Massumi.

Marlowe, C. (1609). *The tragicall history of the horrible life and death of Doctor Faustus.* London: Iohn Wright.

May, G. G. (1982). *Will and spirit: a contemplative psychology.* San Fransisco: Harper & Row.

McFadyen, A. I. (1990). *The call to personhood.* Cambridge: Cambridge University Press.

McIntosh, E. (Ed.) (1964). *The Concise Oxford dictionary of current English* (Fifth ed.). Oxford: Clarendon Press.

McNeill, J. T. (Ed.) (2011). *Calvin: Institutes of the Christian Religion.* Louisville KY: Westminster John Knox Press.

Ovid (Publius Ovidius Naso) (2004). *Metamorphoses: a new verse translation.* London: Penguin. Translated from the Latin by David Raeburn.

Plantigna, A. (1981). Is belief in God properly basic? *Noûs 15*(1), 41-51.

Post, P. and A. L. Molendijk (2010). *Holy Ground: reinventing ritual space in modern Western culture.* Leuven: Peeters.

Quinn, F. (2010, April). The right to choose: existential-phenomenological psychotherapy with primary school-aged children. *Counselling Psychology Review 25*(1), 41-48.

Religious Society of Friends (Quakers) in Britain (2013). *Quaker faith & practice* (Fifth ed.). London: Religious Society of Friends (Quakers) in Britain.

Shelley, P. B. (1917). *The complete poetical works of Percy Bysshe Shelley including materials never before printed in any edition of the poems, edited with textual notes by Thomas Hutchinson.* Oxford: Oxford University Press.

Sister Penelope (1974). *The coming: a study in the Christian faith.* London: Mowbray.

Suttie, I. D. (1935). *The origins of love and hate.* London: Kegan Paul, Trench, Trubner & Co.

Suttie, I. D. (1988). *The origins of love and hate.* London: Free Association.

Tennyson, Lord. A. (1921). *Poems of Tennyson 1829-1868; compiled by Sir H. Warren.* Oxford: Oxford University Press.

Tillich, P. (1962). *The courage to be.* London: Collins.

Washburn, M. (1994). *Transpersonal psychology in psychoanalytic perspective.* Albany NY: State University of New York Press.

Weber, M. (1965). *The sociology of religion.* London: Methuen. Translated by Ephraim Fischoff from the fourth edition of *Wirtschaft und Gesellschaft.*

Wilber, K. (1996). *A brief history of everything.* Boston: Shambhala.

Winnicott, D. W. (1971). *Playing and reality.* London: Tavistock.

Woolridge, D. (2013). *Proleptic spiritual transformation.* Phd, North-West University, Potchefstroom, RSA.

Wordsworth, W. (1970). *Poems by William Wordsworth: selected and edited with an introduction by George Mallaby.* London: Folio Society.

INDEX